LOVE, HONOR AND DISMAY

Love, Honor and Dismay

Elizabeth Harrison

Doubleday & Company, Inc., Garden City, New York, 1977

ISBN: 0-385-12842-8
Library of Congress Catalog Card Number 76–57872
Copyright © 1976 by Elizabeth Harrison and Peter Evans/Atticus
Production
First Edition in the United States of America
Printed in the United States of America

To R.H.

CONTENTS

LOVE, HONOR AND DISMAY

1. The End of the Season

My family took their summer holidays at Dinard on the coast of Brittany, almost too late, when the days were drawing in and the tariffs had been reduced in a last bid to extend the season for a few days more while waiting for winter.

The little town, like a merry-go-round, was slowing down; along the Promenade du Clair de Lune the notices began to appear in the boutiques and bistros: *fin de la saison.* The town seemed to grow as the holiday makers moved on and the big brightly striped umbrellas, slightly faded now, folded one by one on the beach. The pavement cafés moved inside and in the harbor the last of the summer boats bobbed listlessly in the bay.

A sense of serenity settled on the town as the shadows lengthened. It was the time I loved best of all. The sea, so still and green. The local guttural voices gratified at reaching the close of another season. The smell of familiar foods filled the square. The musicians now relaxed, played at last what pleased them.

Yet I was impatient with childhood. Childhood was a land to run through quickly.

The mist was always just about to clear, giving a glimpse of tomorrow, a tomorrow full of possibilities, where don'ts and can'ts were forever banished.

Childhood was full of hushed voices, and sentences abruptly ending as you entered the room, of being constantly told that one's elders knew best and that you would understand when you grew up.

In 1945 I remember overhearing my maternal grandparents saying that my father had a constituency, he had caught it apparently in a place called Croydon.

I wondered if it were painful to have a constituency. How did one get rid of it? When I inquired, all I could glean was that it was a Socialist constituency. They didn't seem too happy, I was informed in tight tones.

"We are all Liberals."

When my parents returned to Wales I was relieved to see they both looked very well. My father seemed particularly cheerful and happy. It was the beginning of many turbulent years of political involvement for my father, and in a sense for the whole household. A little while later I discovered a constituency was not a contagious disease after all.

Childhood was a never-never land which one could visit daily to soothe one's bruised ego, where one was always right and every dream seemed possible. It was a place to bury moments too private and too embarrassing to share with anyone.

My brothers—Gwilym, six years older than me, and Morgan, eighteen months my junior—and I spent a lot of our time in our paternal grandparents' home in Wales. A lovely old Georgian house called Garth Celyn in Bridgend. It stood on the outskirts of the sleepy little market town, with its stables backing onto the main street.

My grandmother, a large ambitious woman, had been cruelly confined to a wheelchair by a number of strokes, thus ending her career in local politics. She now presided over the household with all the determination of a newly elected chairman. She supervised the kitchen staff as they tended the cauldrons of bubbling jam, the bottling of fruit from the orchard and the baking of bread.

At night, the old house creaked and groaned, its uneven floorboards giving away our secret nightly raids to the third floor, which was always locked. My brothers and I imagined all sorts of gruesome deeds being enacted behind that forbidding door.

The large mellow walled garden was full of wonderful hiding places. Sunny corners where the peaches grew against the warm old stone, the crazy-paved little inner courtyard that sported a sundial, which had been weathered by many a storm, the vegetable garden, which lay locked behind a heavy wooden door, was mysterious and out of bounds. It was, therefore, the most desirable place of all.

My grandfather, a tall, thin, gentle man, was a vet. Part of the stables had been converted into a surgery and operating room for sick animals. The smell of disinfectant was always fighting with the honeysuckle and the lavender.

I didn't like my childhood, I never felt at home there. Only later did I realize how Welsh and incendiary it had been, full of the fear of God and hell, and no clear picture of heaven, of lunches that stretched and groaned into holy books and chapel at six. Laughter and loud voices were not encouraged. Wales decreed the need for somber Sundays.

Childhood had the most wonderful thing of all—it had tomorrow.

There is always a moment, looking back, when one realizes that one was finally removed from childhood and life was never quite the same again. Such a moment is seldom reached without a sense of melancholy, however hard one may have pursued it down the years. It is rarely a moment for subtle omens. It certainly wasn't for me. I was just eighteen.

Wound up by the slow mechanism of misgiving and shock, I felt apart from everyone. Despite the cold, I refused to hurry. I walked slowly home along Gloucester Road. Perhaps my drifting demeanor was meant to convince me that my dignity was intact. The snow, which had been falling in heavy flakes for some time, soaked my face. I went over and over in my mind the events of that Friday afternoon in 1955, trying calmly to reconcile my life to fate.

I was in my fifth term at the Royal Academy of Dramatic Art when John Fernald, the principal, summoned me to his study. With no preamble at all, with no soothing words or comforting phrases—but with faultless rhythm and exemplary economy—he informed me that my future as an actress was limited. Indeed, as far as he and the Royal Academy were concerned, it was limited to that afternoon.

Self-confidence (or maybe a little simple narcissism) is necessary to an actress. I had certainly not noticed any dangerous cooling in Mr. Fernald's opinion of my ability, although I was aware that it was never immense. His sudden prophetic vision of my future came as a very nasty shock.

As it says in the Bible, the truth shall make you free.

Nevertheless, even if one goes along with that bit of scriptural stoicism, it was still very short notice to be made quite so free.

I wondered, since he seemed so very positive, whether Mr. Fernald could possibly be right. There were, I knew, some areas of doubt concerning my versatility as an actress. I had to admit, I was not at my best in the classical roles.

When I played Helena in *A Midsummer Night's Dream*, my interpretation at first startled, then simply dumfounded Winnie Ourtan, the director. She summoned the entire class and made them follow my performance line by line. I was line perfect; the trouble was it sounded nothing like Shakespeare.

Miss Ourtan and the class, unable to fix my style with any certainty, seemed reluctant to judge its unusual quality for its own sake. I wonder now whether my performance was far more a symptom of antipathy for the spotty young man playing my love object Demetrius than a failure to come to terms with Shakespeare.

Although, I had to admit, my Cobweb was nothing to write home about. But then again, I really had been awfully good as Sir Peter Teazle in *The School for Scandal*. That had been in the school play, when I was twelve.

Perhaps, I thought as I continued along Gloucester Road, I should concentrate on character parts. Perhaps I was really cut out to be one of those actresses who don't make it until they are over fifty. When you are just eighteen that seems a very long way off.

The outlook was not encouraging. And there were other uncomfortable thoughts. Thoughts about dedication, about discipline and industry and giving one's all for one's art. Admittedly I was seeking to minimize my blame in the catastrophe. No doubt I was somewhat prejudiced on the subject, but certainly laziness could not be imputed to me. Between the hours of 10 A.M. and 6 P.M. I'd done my best. It was between 6 P.M. and 10 A.M. that I may have slipped up.

I simply had a strong natural bias toward social gatherings. I was lumbered with *joie de vivre*. My exuberance demanded a larger stage. Perhaps I needed to be two people at once.

That I had survived so long playing both the drama student and the debutante was no small achievement. It had needed determination, stamina and considerable ingenuity. There were so many things to do; so much was happening. I had spent a year in a convent in Switzerland, and now there seemed so much lost time to make up for. So many parties to go to, so many new people to meet. Sleeping seemed such a waste of time. I firmly believed that the quality of one's life was shaped by cheerful insomnia and an unyielding sense of pleasure. I was blessed with both. Nothing, I felt, was too strenuous for my constitution.

The Season was fun. I had no doubts about that. It may also have been a frivolous, irrelevant and crumbling tradition, but it was a fine and necessary antidote to the exigent routine of RADA. I felt no tiredness at all. I simply couldn't accept that my social life had been the cause of my sudden downfall. Indeed, it had always seemed to me that the Season was simply an extension of my education. Experience can only be gathered by living; I've never yet met a good actor who got it all from early nights and Stanislavski. It was, I recognized, a somewhat limited experience, doing the Season, but experience nonetheless. And I found it entirely to my liking. It was as if one had a foot in two worlds. I had felt the magnificence of the May Ball at Oxford. I knew the romance of candlelight flicker-

ing through the barely moving trees as one strolled in the
park, listening to the distant midnight music. I had seen
the past in those lovely old houses on the nights they returned to their rich ghosts and hard-up heirs for a moment more, before the hordes of visitors came back next
morning at 2/6*d* a time.

I had also fallen in love several times, but always for a
span too short to be painful. Preoccupied with my future
as an actress, I had permitted myself to be spoiled by all
the young men. I had not altogether overlooked the advantages of their indulgences. Fortunately, most of them
were far too indolent ever to bear grudges. There had
been a very dashing lieutenant in the Royal Navy, David
Gunn. My parents were very keen on him, especially
when he called on me decked out in his full ceremonial
uniform and carrying a gold-topped cane. He was so correct, so full of moral rectitude, that his car genuinely
broke down on our way home from the splendid Naval
Ball at Greenwich. Patient, forbearing and resigned, he
pushed me through the streets of South London at dawn,
keeping up a flow of chitchat for all the world as if he
were making polite conversation in my father's drawing
room.

"This is a very old car," I pointed out aloofly after an
hour or so of very slow progress. I was never awfully
clever at avoiding those topics which may irritate.

"Yes," he said, refusing to be drawn on its vintage.
"Isn't it." He endeavored to give the impression of stroll-
ing alongside as he pushed the motor laboriously up a
small but noticeable incline.

"It is possible to buy some very good new cars now," I
said.

"Yes, so I believe," he answered vaguely.

"Foreign sports cars are very nice," I said. "And quite the thing."

"It's odd how one becomes attached to one's old British banger," he replied, breathing strangely. He still endeavored to behave like a rider leading an aged charger after a long last chase.

"Is it raining very hard?" I asked.

"Yes, it is rather," he said. His pleasant smile now seemed to be tempered by a genuine curiosity.

My father thought that he would make a very good match. But he never called upon me again. It didn't really matter. Romantic failures had never bothered me very much. But now this.

Burdened and obsessed by the rejection of that afternoon, I was not aware that a car had been moving slowly alongside me for some distance. The snow was now coming down very hard, and the wind was cutting. There were a very few people on Gloucester Road now. The snow had settled a silence on the street like the silence of a sickroom.

"I said, do you want a lift?"

The driver had wound down his window and was calling to me across the pavement.

He was a good-looking man, smiling, a nice smile that was almost apologetic, almost shy.

"It's no night to be out for a stroll," he said. "I thought you might like a lift."

I stared at him blankly. All my life Mother had warned me never to accept lifts from strangers.

He half opened the door of his car.

"I'm going to Queens Gate," I said, getting in beside him without another moment's hesitation.

"You might have frozen to death before you made it," he said. "My name is Peter Prowse."

"I'm Elizabeth Rees-Williams," I told him.

He was easy to talk to in a pleasant, rather matter-of-fact way. It was warm in the car, an old Daimler with deep worn leather seats and a walnut dashboard; it smelled vaguely of cigarettes and oil. He told me he was an actor.

"I'm an actress," I said. "At least I was . . . until a couple of hours ago." I told him my story, carefully keeping it superficial and cheerfully polite; when you are young you are self-conscious about the intimacies of failure.

He listened quietly, not interrupting at all. I could sense his sympathy. But there was something else, too. He seemed to be trying to make up his mind about something.

When we arrived at my home, he said quickly, "Look, I'm up for the lead in *Winter Journey*. The Clifford Odets play. The auditions are tonight. I know they are still looking for a girl to play the ingenue. . . . If you're at all interested, I could take you along and introduce you to the director."

"Thank you, how awfully kind. Yes, I am interested," I said, thinking I should have accepted lifts from strangers more often. I silently wished that it had been a character part they had been casting instead of an ingenue. A role in which I could have lost myself beneath pots of paint and a heavy accent. I was now firmly convinced that my destiny lay in the Grand Dame of the character actress.

Peter Prowse picked me up at nine o'clock sharp. I found it easy to talk to this large, strongly built man; his straight blond hair kept flopping over his forehead. The audition, he told me as we headed west across London on the hard settled snow, was being held at a coffee bar in Earls Court. Earls Court is not a location one readily associates with West End productions, or first-class managements, and something of this thought must have appeared on my face.

Peter gave me a reassuring grin. He said, "It's a West End production all right. The director is a very young man, new in the business. He's going to use this place for casting and rehearsals." I had a feeling that the production was rather more in competition than in association with H. M. Tennants. That was fine with me. I didn't think the Establishment Theatre was quite ready for me anyway.

Earls Court, although only a five-minute drive from my home in Queens Gate, was totally different. Queens Gate was spacious, formal, impersonal and hushed. It was essentially residential; private cars only, not a hint of trade. Earls Court was full of life with coffee bars where people spilled over onto the pavements; pubs with open doors and noisy customers, and sandwich stands with old tea urns. Students restless with their small bed-sitters wandered aimlessly around the street.

We arrived at the Troubadour coffee bar. I didn't know what to expect. It was warm, cozy, dimly lit. It seemed to be full of young people, mostly art students. The dry stone walls were whitewashed and hung with crude farm implements, oxen yokes, ancient locks and massive iron keys. The whole place was candlelit—a single white household candle to each small scrubbed pine table. The guttering candles threw odd deformed shadows against the littered walls, fragmented shapes fitted together like an abstract, turbulent jigsaw puzzle. In a far dark corner, somebody was strumming a guitar, going over and over the same melancholy chords, with no intricacy at all. The place was crowded; it seemed to be a close community.

The Troubadour was owned and run by a young Canadian couple in their early twenties, Sheila and Michael

Van Bloeman. They helped hungry out-of-work actors, homeless musicians and aspiring artists. They supported in their own fashion numerous students of the arts. The Van Bloemans only had limited means themselves, but in their way they were the modern Patron of the Arts, but I am running ahead. . . .

Peter clutched my hand and led me to a table occupied by one man. This man had his head bent low, reading a book, an uncommonly large book, by the glow of the single candle. All I could see as we approached the table was an unruly mass of red hair falling almost to his broad shoulders. Because of the uncertain light of that place, he seemed to emerge from a dark mass, an enormous body, a body with a tense quality that did not go with reading.

There was an air about this stranger that made me nervous, apprehensive; we had seated ourselves at his table before he looked up from his book. He looked directly at me without speaking and without smiling. It was a face intensely alive. His eyes, red-rimmed and heavy from lack of sleep, were blue and artfully alert in his pale face. He reminded me strongly of someone; much later I realized that he looked just like Van Gogh's "Portrait of the Artist."

"This is Richard Harris," said Peter Prowse.

We stared at each other.

"Richard, Elizabeth Rees-Williams."

He gave me a curt nod, but still no smile. I felt uncomfortable; I felt overdressed. I knew my own smile had gone wrong somewhere between leaving my eyes and reaching my mouth.

Suddenly Richard got to his feet—I was astonished to see they were naked. In an incredibly swift movement for such a large man, he disappeared downstairs into the cellar, beckoning Peter to follow him.

Alone at the small table I began to feel the miserable insecurity of neglect; it did nothing for my confidence, which I was sorely in need of as I waited to be auditioned. After a long time—it seemed like a *very* long time —I was summoned to the cellar. It was lit by a single bare bulb. A few wooden chairs and a wooden table stood on the cold stone floor. The atmosphere was inquisitorial. Richard sat behind the table. Without standing up he handed me a few pages of script and asked me to read the role of the ingenue.

"Here, read here. The girl."

It was the first time I'd heard him speak. I was surprised by his quiet Irish brogue.

The scene he gave me to read was where the young girl, abused by the star of the show, has hysterics. Since I was rapidly heading in that direction myself anyway, I suppose I gave an adequate performance.

A week later, Richard telephoned to tell me I had the part.

The next weeks were hectic, exhausting, often unnerving and full of surprises. I was astonished to learn, among other things, that Richard—my first impresario and director—was still a student at the London Academy of Music and Dramatic Art. That set me back a bit.

And not only had he put money into the production— he had put *all* his money into the production and nobody else's. After only six months at LAMDA—"Anxious to get moving and try out some of my own ideas"—he had used up his entire savings to hire the tiny Irving Theatre just off Leicester Square for a limited season of *Winter Journey*. (The day we moved out, striptease moved in, and it has never been legitimate since.)

I continued to lead, just as I had led at RADA, a double life. As a debutante, I was in the middle of doing the Season, traveling the canapé circuit. It explains, I suppose, my exhaustion during those weeks of *Winter Journey* rehearsals; certainly my role was not *that* demanding, I must admit.

Rehearsals were usually in the evenings (the director, of course, had to attend classes during the day) and I would frequently arrive straight from some cocktail party or another. But I was learning all the time. Now I had the sense to slip into a duffel coat and leave my mother's old fur in the back of some boy friend's MG before walking into the Troubadour. I was learning to blend.

I was also learning that people were not always polite, tactful, obliging, well behaved and complaisant. And men were not always chivalrous. I discovered that people lost their tempers, swore, shouted, wept, threw things and often each other. This world was in utter contrast to the world I had inhabited for the last eighteen years. I was both appalled and fascinated by it.

Richard had cast Peter Prowse in the lead, but as rehearsals progressed it became clear that director and leading man had different ideas how the role should be played. Richard, his own money in the show, displayed all the fanaticism of his rashness, a facet of his character I was to become familiar with. Richard never doubted his own wisdom. He never lacked the courage to follow through his chosen course, no matter how daunting the odds. Peter, ambitious and strong-willed, pointed out that it was impossible to give an authoritative performance without some of his own fanaticism coming through.

People said it would be all right on the night. I was inexperienced enough to believe it. I genuinely believed that through some strange alchemy an audience contributed that last ingredient that turned a poor dress rehearsal into a brilliant opening night.

There were the usual number of unplanned dramas; blown lines, misplaced props, lighting mistakes and missed cues. Actors expect such things on these occasions. What we didn't know—and had no way of knowing—was that our director would play such a vivid leading role, obtrusive as it was dramatic.

During the entire performance, he paced up and down the narrow aisle in the auditorium; he punctuated our speeches with sharp intakes of breath, like a man recovering from a marathon race lost; furious hissing sounds emanated from his lips every time a line or a gesture was not delivered to his liking. He would utter curses so audible that heads swiveled his way with the clockwork precision of a Centre Court crowd at Wimbledon.

My father remembers that opening night very well.

"Richard," he recounted long afterward, when asked about that production, "had his shirt hanging out of his trousers. Out of the *seat* of his trousers. The only time I've ever seen that."

Richard continued to give his remarkable display on the aisle during the entire two-week run.

I had now known Richard for six weeks and in that time we had never had any private conversations or been alone together for a moment. Neither of us sought each other's company. We seemed, on the face of it, utterly incompatible. I suppose, more than anything else, I was afraid that he would despise me and my way of life, my background and friends. The feeling was no more than an intuitive wariness on my part; Richard had never mentioned anything remotely to do with my private life, had never asked what I did when I was away from the theater. Later he told me that when he discovered I was a debutante daughter of a Peer he was absolutely furious.

Fortunately, I had no idea that my position in the company was so precarious. The day he learned that I was a deb—and a deb actively doing the Season at that—he told the cast that he planned to get rid of me.

He announced, "The first time she's so much as two minutes late for rehearsal, she's out on her social arse."

For a man with so much antagonism in him, he hid his displeasure and intent very well. I truly had no idea that Mr. Fernald's prophecy was so close to fulfillment. He seemed barely to notice me, although I was always uneasily aware of him. Only later did I shudder to think how my whole future hung on minutes and fast MGs. The play survived its limited run and audience. I was surprised to find how much of my life it had occupied; I now felt an emptiness.

The morning after the final curtain I returned to the theater for the last time. I felt a dull ache spread through my entire body as I suddenly realized I probably would never see Richard again. Until that moment I hadn't realized I wanted to see him again. The whole place still seemed to be so full of him, his presence, his vitality and energy.

I went to my dressing room. He was standing there. His back was to the door and he was rearranging things on my dressing table in that endlessly fussy way that people have when they are waiting for something to happen.

"Hello, what are you doing here?" he said, turning quickly.

"I've come to collect my bits and pieces." I was too overcome to ask what *he* was doing there, in *my* dressing room. We talked about a lot of things, none of them important and some of them silly. I suddenly realized that I had never heard Richard talk about anything but the play before. That play had obsessed him, and challenged him, all the hours and weeks I'd known him. Now it was over. Still he wasn't relaxed.

At last he said, "Would you like to come with me to Essex? To visit me cousins."

It wasn't exactly the most romantic invitation I'd had, but it certainly was the most irresistible. I accepted, and immediately asked whether he would like to take me to a film premiere I'd been given tickets for.

"And I'll take you to dinner afterward," he said with a gallantry that pleased and surprised me.

Although unaware of his aggressive opinion of me, I suspected that he would hardly cast himself in the role of Deb's Delight.

I still had no idea how utterly different our worlds were then. His idea of dinner after the show was a very far cry from my idea of what that meant.

I was surprised, after the premiere, when he said he had not booked a table anywhere. I suggested a nightclub that I knew fairly well.

"Okay," he said. "Right you are."

He behaved impeccably and with fine humor.

"You would think," he said, pointing to the swizzle sticks on our table, their tops wrapped in brightly colored paper. "You would think in a posh place like this they would be able to afford real flowers."

I laughed and thought warmly what an amusingly original fellow he was, little realizing he was perfectly serious.

I ordered.

"I'll have that," he said.

I ordered again.

"I'll have some of that, too," he said.

I ordered once more.

"I'll have just a little of that, too," he said.

How lovely it was to be eating the same food, enjoying the same taste sensations; he was such a romantic.

Months later he told me he couldn't understand "the bloody menu." And it was the first time he had eaten veal in his life. We avoided French restaurants for quite a while after that. And it wasn't only the language that inhibited us. Richard had spent his entire rent and food money for two weeks on that one dinner.

2. A Kind of Madness

Our next dinner together was not so grand. Richard had gone to endless trouble to ensure its success. There was complete willingness on my part to be seduced, modestly unproclaimed by me, and curiously unsuspected by Richard. Still it wasn't easy.

Richard was at that time gypsying around London, bedding down each night wherever he could; sometimes this meant a bench on the Embankment.

He occasionally shared a single room in Nevern Place off West Cromwell Road with Robert Young and Len Taylor. Young was an actor who sometimes washed up and played the guitar at the Troubadour; Taylor was on the threshold of a career in advertising. It was to Nevern Place that Richard invited me to dinner.

I had no inkling of the efforts he had gone to. Not only had he secured the room for the evening, he had made Young and Taylor swear on their mothers' lives that they would not return before midnight.

Young's absence was not merely a matter of discretion but of some culinary urgency, too. Richard had persuaded

Sheila and Michael Van Bloeman, of the Troubadour, to prepare him a dinner he could take home. "It's important," he told them, admitting he was for the moment unable to pay for it. "I'm entertaining, you see." He was especially adept, even then, at conveying what really mattered to him without revealing himself at all.

The meal, wrapped in silver foil, was deposited between the blankets on Robert Young's bed.

When I arrived, Richard popped a couple of eggs into a tin kettle on the single gas ring in the corner. "Dinner will be ready in three minutes," he announced airily. He poured me a glass of chilled white wine from a bottle he had dangling on a string from the windowsill. The room was threadbare and exhausted from the years and rebuffs of precarious lettings. It made no real effort to be a bed-sitting room; it was a bedroom, a bedroom for men. Two single narrow beds ran parallel along the side walls. The narrow curtains were made for a smaller window than the bay they now adorned. The carpet was too thin to offer warmth or comfort, and the brown linoleum had long ago passed the point where protection might be considered prudent.

The eggs were ready.

Richard lowered the gas jet with a lot of squinting, crouching calculation and a series of critical-looking gourmet-gauged adjustments.

"There," he said, turning quickly to the bed.

Expecting by now only a three-minute egg dinner, I was agreeably surprised by his sudden revelation: the Van Bloeman meal (steak, fried bananas wrapped in bacon, baked potatoes) nesting in the warm Witney depths of Robert Young's bed.

"I cooked this earlier," he said carelessly. Perhaps trying to impress me still further, he added: "In the kettle."

"Kettles are very useful things," I said.

Since I had never cooked a meal in my life, I didn't doubt for a second that he had concocted the entire dinner in the kettle. I didn't think it was very clever or particularly extraordinary. Although I was soon to learn that nothing he ever did was ordinary; in his presence the commonplace became baffling, and the baffling seemed perfectly ordinary.

It did occur to me later, on my way home, that his choice of hot plate was rather primitive; probably, I concluded, it was an Irish tradition.

Anyway it made for such a lovely warm bed.

Our relationship grew intense at an astonishing rate. It unnerved and consumed both of us. One is vulnerable in the beginning of a love affair. We decided to see each other only on alternate days in a genuine bid to put a brake on our emotions. I wanted to see Richard all the time. Only with the most determined effort did I keep up with my own social life.

I continued to join weekend house parties in the country, but now they had lost a great deal of their fascination for me. My frantic imagination lingered with Richard in Earls Court. Curiously, I can still recall those weekends with clarity.

I cannot be exact about the date, but it was somewhere between the time old-family snobbery went into decline and working-class chic began to flourish.

Actors were now proudly claiming working-class connections. *Look Back in Anger*, written by John Osborne in 1956, did much more than offer a marvelous part to a young actor called Kenneth Haig. It opened up endless opportunities to actors to play roles, classical and otherwise, that they would never have been considered for. The image of the actor changed almost overnight. The

Angry Young Man was in; the elegant eloquent dandy was out.

Years later I remember Rex Harrison telling me that when he started in the theater, at the age of sixteen, actors had to ape gentlemen. If an actor had a working-class accent he was confined to playing servants or members of the lower order.

This turn in the tide in the theatrical world came at a perfect moment for Richard. His looks, manners and acting were all of the new school. Vigorous, volatile and unpredictable.

I was enjoying both worlds, but I was not committed to either. I was spending the weekend with the Brudenells, direct descendants of the Earl of Cardigan, at their country seat, Deene Park, in Northamptonshire. The high point of the weekend was the Hunt Ball and the convivial Edmund Brudenell and his sister Philippa were entertaining a large house party. It seemed to me then that every person present was related to the Upper House. I had only just arrived and was enjoying a sherry before lunch when I became acutely aware that a fellow guest was staring at me most intently. He was a tall, bony young man with sandy hair who had been talking animatedly when I first entered the room about his "wedgement and the enswmuth cotht of stabling." But now he had gone silent and was heavily into the staring game. I returned his gaze with as much equanimity as I could muster. At last he said seriously, "I say, you're the daughter of the Socialist Peer, aren't you?"

I admitted I was.

He continued to stare as if I were a lady of positively no birth at all. He seemed surprised that I was actually built more or less along the lines of the other women in the room.

"Well," he said in an indignant voice, "I've never met a Socialist before."

As far as I was concerned he still hadn't. However, I saw no reason to put him out of his misery. I think he actually feared that I might give him some dreadful Socialist disease.

My family have always been Liberal, a fact that never preoccupied me then and has failed to concern me since. It is true that my father strayed from the Liberal fold for a time when he became a Socialist MP in 1945. He was defeated in 1950 and elevated to the peerage by Clement Attlee.

Life with my parents had been full of rapid changes. In politics, as in the theater, the future was unpredictable. Constituents, like audiences, play their role. My father had risen quickly from Parliamentary Under-Secretary of State for Commonwealth Relations to Minister of Civil Aviation.

Repressed by motives of good breeding, my hosts appeared not to hear my brief exchange with the bony young man, just as they appeared not to notice that the guest of honor that weekend, Cecil Woodham-Smith, had recently written *The Reason Why*, a less than flattering account of Lord Cardigan's role in the Charge of the Light Brigade.

The lunch that day was amusing, prolonged. Grandeur, as well as impeccable manners, is part of the Brudenell heritage: they accept gold plate as most of us accept the Delft. That day I had the distinct impression that the footmen rather outnumbered the guests. There was, too, an air of lovely eccentricity about the house as well as the family. My bedroom was vast and regal and warmed by a massive log fire that a functionary maintained throughout my stay; the linen was crisp and smelled of lavender.

Rich tapestries covered the walls and the casement windows looked out upon the most magnificent park.

"Incidentally, whatever you do, don't turn left when you leave your bedroom," old man Brudenell said casually at lunch. "The house has rather fallen down a bit on that side. A very nasty drop. Open to the elements. Never turn left. You'll always be safe if you turn to the right."

George Brudenell, Edmund and Philippa's father, was seventy-five then. He was a portly gentleman with an old-century courtesy, and engagingly vague. He did not appear very often and when he did it was with an almost spectral air. Wrapped in a vast Inverness cape, he appeared after lunch from his quarters in some unvisited part of the house and suggested a walk in the grounds. I had noticed one young man at lunch. He was one of the most handsome men I had ever seen in my life. His hair was blond, his nose straight and aristocratic. His eyes were very blue. As we strolled behind the evanescent Brudenell, I noticed that the beautiful young man was changing significantly. After half an hour or so his complexion had become profusely blotched. His nose had swollen to twice its normal size and turned to a plummy shade of purple. His cheeks had taken on a distinctly gorged and aged look.

I realized that he was in the middle of a severe attack of hay fever; the poor boy could barely see but stumbled on without a murmur. I was most impressed. Nobody mentioned his affliction at all.

He did not appear at the dance that evening, nor indeed did I see him ever again.

There is nothing quite as lovely as a perfect English summer's evening; the air was soft and the night richly textured. The house had been floodlit and all the windows opened out onto the deep terraces. The whole occasion had the almost unreal air of a slow ritualistic ballet. We danced until dawn.

Only the following morning, awakened by a footman bearing a breakfast on a vast tray filled with inviting silver-dome-topped dishes, did the small awful doubts begin: Christ! Did I go too far last night? What was I saying? I hope it wasn't what I think I said.

Later, in the morning room, you meet again that devastating young man who danced and danced with you, and made you laugh so much, and walked with you in the moonlight. Without the moonlight, you think, he really isn't quite so much. Alas, you know he is thinking exactly the same thoughts about you.

My parents were beginning to suspect that perhaps I had an intense interest in my life that was not altogether confined to my pursuit of the arts. They had been understanding, if somewhat reluctant, about my theatrical ambitions. They had promised that if I went to a finishing school in Switzerland for a year, I could audition for RADA on my return.

In the fifties it wasn't considered particularly desirable for a girl to work. My mother said hopefully, from time to time, that if I felt I wanted to do something, then why not something useful like a nurse? The sight of blood makes me faint and I felt I would be more of a liability than an asset to the medical profession.

My parents were tolerant as I continued my search for work. I played a small part in Arthur Miller's *All My Sons* in a theater club in London. I was delighted when I was told to report to the studios for filming with a commercial film company.

"Don't worry about the script," my agent assured me.

"You'll pick it up as you go along." He was right. I didn't have any lines. I spent the entire time being securely strapped to the seat of a skidding car. I was silently, but expressively, illustrating the benefits of a safety belt.

I landed a job as assistant stage manager and juvenile lead at Warrington Rep (twice nightly, a new production every week). My theatrical hopes soared but my heart sank; the idea of leaving Richard upset me tremendously. In reality it wasn't so bad. Twice-nightly rep is not a business to encourage a lot of introspection.

I arrived in Warrington late on a Sunday evening and spent several hours lugging my suitcase through the less salubrious parts of town looking for digs. At 11 P.M., exhausted and still without a roof over my head, I walked into the police station. The duty sergeant listened to my tale of woe and gave me one more address to try.

"If you don't have any luck there, lass, come back and I'll find you a cell for the night," he said in a broad warm Lancashire accent.

This time I was lucky. I was offered a bed in the front room of a family who worked at the local soap factory.

Rep, I quickly discovered, was hard work. Every Monday morning I was up at the crack of dawn (long before the soap workers stirred) to load my handcart with the props I had managed to borrow from various shops for the previous week's production. These had to be safely returned by 10 A.M. so that I could get to the theater in time for the first read-through of our next production. After a break for high tea at 4:30 P.M., we would begin our first evening performance at 6 P.M.; the second house went up at 8:30. I was usually home by 11 P.M. Then I had to study my lines for the following day. All this for seven pounds a week; the soap workers were appalled.

"It's sweated labor, miss," the eldest son of the house told me. He had a political bent and talked to me a great deal about the Factory Acts of 1833. It was, it seemed, a favorite topic of his. "You should have inspectors in those halls, miss. Inspectors'll put a stop to it soon enough."

But I loved it. Although I missed Richard terribly, I was having a marvelous time. The audiences didn't expect any great performances and certainly never got any. Yet everyone seemed content. We had to act our way through the incessant rustle of paper bags, and the disturbingly tempting smell of fish and chips, during the matinees, when it appeared to be the local custom to combine the show with a late lunch or early tea.

When it all got too much I would catch the midnight train to London on Saturday, arriving at Euston at six in the morning, spending Sunday with Richard and returning on the midnight train, arriving in Warrington just in time to wheel my wheelbarrow. . . .

It was a rough, exhilarating, wearing, invaluable experience. When my contract ended, I returned to London with genuinely mixed feelings.

Richard was still at LAMDA, and continuing to live a vagrant hand-to-mouth existence. This was partly due to his instinctive dislike of landladies, with whom he had a bond of incompatibility and distrust. But mostly his incessant mobility was inspired by a chronic shortage of money.

Some nights he was still reduced to a bench on the Embankment; sometimes when the weather was really bad he would spend 2/6d. on a dormitory bed in a South London doss house. Guests at this establishment were so poor and desperate, he slept in all his clothes, including shoes. "If you removed as much as a dirty handkerchief from your pocket somebody would steal it by morning," he said.

He had forfeited his most dependable refuge, Robert Young's room in Nevern Place, due to a piece of unfortunate timing. A vivid and somewhat inclement impersonation of Young's landlady, staged in the local pub, was overheard by the lady herself, quietly sipping warm gin in the adjacent snuggery.

"And you, Mr. Harris," she said, snapping back the sliding partition between snuggery and public bar at the end of his exuberant performance, "you can piss off out of my house right now, and never come back."

Richard's nomad life style and summary sleeping arrangements had a number of obvious disadvantages for young lovers. It was apparent to me that if we were to continue our affair in any kind of civilized style, more permanent lodging arrangements would have to be made quickly.

Since Richard's immediate appearance and latent hostility toward landladies were sorely against him, I took on the job of finding a suitable room to rent. "Try," advised Richard, "to get a long lease on something. Try to get at least a couple of weeks."

It wasn't easy. I traipsed the length and breadth of Earls Court, knocking on doors, inspecting dank basements and leaking attics, ignoring the "No Coloureds," "No Irish Need Apply" tags scrawled beneath the "Room to Let" signs in the newsagents' windows.

We went through a series of rooms; the precise occupancy usually depended upon the length of time I could keep Richard and the landlady from converging. Our departure almost invariably followed such confrontations.

We spent our days making love (my mother insisted I

should be home by 10 P.M., and as long as I obeyed that rule she never inquired about my days), playing Stan Kenton records and reading. Sometimes Richard worked on his poems.

He made me aware of writers like Joyce and Yeats, he taught me how to appreciate the humor of O'Casey. He read aloud from Dylan Thomas, whom he admired; he had visited every stone and hollow, every tree and corner and coal-pitted town Thomas had ever written about.

As well as being my lover, Richard was a mentor, a teacher. Until I met him I had no idea of the pleasures of learning.

My education had been rather discordant and slightly incongruous. I had been to nine schools of varying denominations (Catholic, Quaker, Church of England) and social shades (Welsh Comprehensive, Swiss Finishing School, Secondary Modern in my father's Croydon constituency). This was no doubt excellent in helping one to get used to meeting strangers; it probably made one fairly tolerant of other people's problems, opinions and philosophies. But it didn't instill in one a sense of academic continuity or curiosity.

Now I was being stimulated intellectually as well as emotionally. I felt good. But our fortunes were slipping. When he was obliged to move to yet another sleazy back room (they were definitely going downhill, a fact that was becoming evident even to us) I grew quietly anxious. My £50 dress allowance, which I had been using for the necessary deposits on his rooms, was dwindling fast.

"I thought last time we had reached rock bottom," I said wryly.

"This is the bottom of the fucking barrel, all right," Richard said, looking round his new home.

The sense of despair in that room was palpable; the damp showed through the peeling wallpaper in dark ugly stains.

"We can't go on like this," I said. "We have to do something."

"Yes," Richard said. His voice was flat.

"What are we going to do with our lives?" I said. I had my own ideas; it seemed so very obvious, but Richard only shrugged.

I said, "Perhaps we could stay together . . . get somewhere more permanent."

He said, "Get married, you mean? Is that what you're saying?"

"Well, yes."

He was very good about it. He accepted me without my having to press the invitation.

Having settled the question of our engagement in our own minds, we now had to convince others of our intent— mainly our parents. It was a tricky situation: I was still under age, and Richard was barely the other side of consent. Moreover, my parents had only a very vague impression of Richard and that was based on his emotional ragged performance on the opening night of *Winter Journey*. They didn't know I was seeing him every single day; they had no idea that I was utterly and completely in love with him.

Richard transmitted an enormous sense of energy. He seemed inextinguishably alive. I felt other men were shallow by comparison. When I had been taken out in the past, I had enjoyed the anticipation, deciding what to wear, how to fix my hair. I had enjoyed the fun of flirtation, I relished the teasing. Now suddenly that had gone; the intensity of my feelings for Richard transcended sensual pleasures and conceits. I didn't care what I wore or how I looked: I was unaware to a degree of me. I simply wanted to be near him. But such emotions are not necessarily the emotions with which to convince one's parents that one has made a wise and proper choice. The Greeks commiserate with those in love; love is a kind of madness, they say. They have a point.

I persuaded my mother to invite Richard to dinner on the following Thursday. Richard had a boisterous anxiety about meeting my father. He pinned a message to the LAMDA notice board asking for help and information on the social etiquette of dining with a Peer of the Realm. Particularly he wanted to know how one should address my father: "Is it," he inquired, "Our Lord? Your Lordship? M'Lud? Sire? Or perhaps plain Baron Ogmore?"

I didn't know it then but it was an attitude of Richard's. On the one hand he wanted to boast of his social involvement, and at the same time put down the Establishment.

The appointed Thursday came. At four o'clock I got a frantic call from Richard.

"I can't come, Liz. I can't come to dinner tonight."

"Why?" I asked nervously.

"Me suit. It's in the cleaners, you see. In the bloody cleaners, and Jesus, wouldn't you know, the bloody place is closed."

It was Thursday, of course. Half day.

He said, "All I have is me jeans."

Sartorially ahead of his time, Richard's jeans were not what the well-dressed young man was wearing that year—and certainly not what he would choose for the introductory dinner with his prospective father-in-law.

I told my parents that Richard had to rehearse late. The dinner was postponed until the following evening.

The doorbell rang at seven o'clock sharp. I sat perfectly motionless in that frozen state of counterfeit composure, waiting for Hughsie, our maid, to open the door. She had been with us for a long time and was not as fast on her feet as she once was, which was not immensely nippy in the first place. This was due not so much to her advancing years as to her extraordinary habit of buying shoes several sizes too large; this gave her the unusual appearance of walking into her shoes rather than in them. She was a large-boned thin lady with short gray hair and two great passions in her life: one was the Friends of the Sunday Baptists Society, and the other was listening to Sandy MacPherson, the BBC organist. Apart from that she was quite steady.

I heard her slowly shuffling along the corridor in her roomy footwear, open the front door . . . and almost at once close it again. She came slowly back along the corridor to the kitchen, then back again to the front door.

"There you are, boy," she said, thrusting the week's dirty laundry into Richard's arms.

The fact that, despite his newly cleaned and pressed suit and borrowed necktie, she had mistaken him for the laundry boy was not the most auspicious start to the evening.

Dinner seemed to last a very long time; it was one of those interminable evenings punctuated with false animation and conversations that start brightly and lapse quickly. After dinner we returned to the drawing room. My mother had an air of worried remoteness. Richard sat on the window seat. His attempt at nonchalance was considerably impaired the moment he crossed his legs. It might have been an elegant enough pose had he not forgotten to put his socks on. Without preamble, he launched into the object of the evening.

"I've got this house in Limerick, you see. And it brings in six pounds a week. And me auntie left me a few shares in Guinness, although I've sold most of those to pay me LAMDA fees, you see. But then I can earn something in the theater, most weeks anyway. . . ."

My father listened with commendable calm, his lawyer's mind making what he could of this sudden, rambling, unforeseen prospectus.

"Are you trying to say you wish to marry my daughter, young man?"

"Yes, I am. I am."

My mother, who had been listening intently and with only the merest change of color as she caught the drift of Richard's conversation, now let out a loud and pitiable wail which grew fainter but no less harrowing as she rushed from the drawing room and down the long corridor to her bedroom. Her histrionic departure left the rest of us in a very uneasy silence.

"Yes, I am," Richard said again, bravely attempting to establish some conversational continuity as if nothing very untoward had happened.

My father as a young man had dabbled in the theater. Like choirs, Amateur Dramatics in Wales were very popular. He had written a play, which was performed in Cardiff, complete with musical accompaniment. His favorite Dickensian character, who made him chuckle aloud, was the actor in *Pickwick Papers*, Alfred Jingle Esq., of No Hall, Nowhere. In retrospect I think my father had a reluctant sympathy, if not always patience, with my passions for the modern-day Jingle.

My mother, on the other hand, worried about my future. One morning as we drove past some of the less desirable residences in North Kensington which advertised "Rooms to Let," she became upset.

"I couldn't bear it if you have to live in one of these places," she said.

I remember still I felt the frisson of apprehension.

My father's permission was given. However, it was agreed that the engagement was to be kept secret until after my father had received a Burmese decoration, the Order of Agga Maha Thray Sithy of Burma. My father had organized a family gathering to celebrate the occasion. After he and Lord Louis Mountbatten had been presented with the award at a ceremony at the Burmese Embassy, the whole Rees-Williams clan, most of whom had traveled up from Wales for the occasion, gathered for dinner. We are a fairly typical Welsh family, which means that every member wants and expects to be fully informed of all the goings-on of every other member. This information is treated in many ways. It is frowned upon sometimes, gossiped over nearly always, then forgotten or made timeless in family legend. They were, therefore, the Rees-Williams throng, extremely inquisitive, not to say bothered, about the young Irishman in their midst. Why was he at a family gathering? Who was he? Where did he come from? And where did he fit in? But we were under strict instructions—this was to be Father's night—and no explanation was offered. When our engagement was officially announced forty-eight hours later, a wry dim view was taken of our enigmatic conduct that evening. Our mum demeanor was put down to the doubtful goings-on they understood took place among people in the stage world.

Shortly after our engagement, Richard had a stroke of good luck. He was having a drink one night in a pub with the poet Desmond O'Grady, from Limerick. Richard overheard someone saying that Joan Littlewood was casting for Brendan Behan's play *The Quare Fellow* at the Theatre Workshop, Stratford East. He borrowed some coins for the telephone from O'Grady and called the theater immediately. He got through to Gerry Raffles, the manager.

"There's only one part we haven't cast yet," Raffles told him. "How old are you?"

Richard said he was twenty-five. Raffles said, "No good. This part is for an old man, a fifty-year-old."

"I give you my word," Richard said, "I look fifty. Easily. I haven't had a good meal for months. I haven't slept for days. Just let me come and see you. Just take a look at me."

Raffles said, "Be here at ten tomorrow morning. I'll see you then."

Raffles was impressed enough with Richard's avowed appearance of premature old age to give him a copy of the script to read. Richard was never a good reader. He stumbled his way through a few pages, becoming increasingly aware that he was not getting through to Raffles at all. He felt the part slipping away from him.

Raffles interrupted. "Perhaps," he suggested too coldly for Richard's tastes, "you would care to try an improvisation if the script is too difficult."

Richard was convinced he had lost the part. He had nothing to lose. He started to improvise a scene at a bar in which he was talking to a man about the audition he had just been too. . . .

"I've wasted my morning and my tube fare auditioning for a cold insensitive bastard. A man with no imagination at all, a fellow with no compassion and no understanding. Wouldn't you know such a man would turn me down." And so on. Richard never, even then, had any lack of self-assurance. As he developed the improvisation his anger grew. He had reached a crescendo of crude eloquence concerning Mr. Raffles when he was stopped dead in his tracks by the sound of one person applauding. From the dark at the back of the stalls walked the figure of Joan Littlewood, still applauding.

"I think," she said to Gerry Raffles, "we've found our Mickser." To Richard she said, "The part is yours. Start Monday. Six weeks. Fifteen pounds a week."

He sins grandly, Richard, but he has always had that redeeming air of a villain who is about to go straight at any moment.

Now, with real money to play with, we started thinking seriously about a place to live, somewhere more tenable than the squalid single rooms in which we had spent our recent past, those long loving days and limited nights. We found a one-room flat in Paddington. It was tiny, with a curtained-off kitchen and our own bathroom. It was clean, dry, and £6 a week. The wedding was arranged for February 9. Before then I was to go to Ireland to meet his family for Christmas.

I had heard so much about Overdale, the large family home in Limerick. Richard had woven a spell about that house, about the whole town. It was both extraordinary and familiar to me. I recognized the streets where he had run as a child, and the trees he had climbed, the hills he had scaled. I knew the school where he had been instructed but barely educated by blameless Jesuits: "They offered me an education and I didn't avail myself of it," he explained so many times. I visited remembered stores and saw old familiar faces I had never seen before. There was his father's flour mill where he had led the strike against his own father for better wages. There was the rugby field on which he had won his junior province cap. The field, a place still of wonder and deep wounds, where he might have been chosen to play for Ireland. Only he got TB at seventeen and that put an end to that.

Then there was Richard's room.

It was the room they put me in that first Christmas.

🌹 🌹 🌹

3. Wedlock

I already knew that room better than any room I had ever had of my own. Every crack in the ceiling, every creaking floorboard was familiar to me.

Richard had spent two years in that room.

He didn't go to a sanatorium when he got tuberculosis; TB was thought to be a shameful disease in those days and his mother didn't want it known that her son had it. So that room had been his cell, his hospital ward, his university. Probably the most important two years of his life were spent in semi-solitude in that room.

Isolated, childhood friendships and passions faltering and dropping away as the months went by, Richard grew strong. His spirit and his imagination soared in that room that was now, for a moment, my room. He retreated deeper and deeper into himself, into books, into poetry and stories. It was the beginning, too, of his quirky essential need for privacy; he remains to this day an inaccessible man.

Overdale had that special aura of adventure and fan-

tasy that only a large house filled with many children
(Richard was the middle son in a family of eight) can
have. How many times had that back garden been a desert, a swamp, an ocean? How many times had the ban-
isters been Niagara Falls, the Matterhorn, some dangerous
downhill ski run? There was a sort of excitement, the excitement perhaps of childhood's lingering secrets, in every
corner of that house. The splendid fantasies of childhood
clung on like friendly ghosts haunting a mock battle-
field.

But it was Richard's room that held the real mystique
for me. It was where his childhood ended. My first Christmas at Overdale taught me a great deal about Richard,
about the problem of being the middle son in a large family, about what made him the kind of man he was—and
the kind of man he was still to become.

I also learned about Dickie.

Richard has never been allowed into Ireland and
Dickie has never left it. His friends and family are very
possessive about Dickie. Richard was a foreigner to them,
a man they did not know or care about.

His family and friends in Limerick couldn't have cared
less about the theater or the movies. They were amused
by Dickie's stories about London and the strange people
he knew in that place, but they felt nothing at all for
Richard, the man who lived there.

During the London run of *The Quare Fellow*, Arthur
Miller saw the play. He was impressed with Richard's
bravura performance and asked him to play the part of a
longshoreman in his new play, *A View from the Bridge*.

It was a controversial play for its time. The Lord
Chamberlain's office particularly objected to one scene in
which the leading man, Anthony Quayle, has to kiss a
young man on the lips. It was a vital point in the plot and

Miller refused to cut the scene or rewrite it. After a great deal of argument, it was decided to turn the Comedy Theatre into a private members' club for the run of the play. It was a stunningly simple maneuver but it successfully avoided the Lord Chamberlain's authority. It was the beginning of the end of censorship in the British theater.

Shortly after the opening of this play we were married. We had gone to a great deal of trouble to find a suitable church. The exact qualifications that would make a church suitable were difficult to define. What it really amounted to was a Catholic church that didn't look like a Catholic church to the Welsh, and a Catholic church that looked like a Catholic church to the Irish.

This hallowed hybrid, naturally enough, was not easy to discover. We finally settled on the Church of Notre Dame in Leicester Square, but quickly learned the truth of the remark that you can't fool all of the people all of the time. I have some very dear great-aunts now in their eighties who are fondly known as the three Bs of Bridgend: Bess, Bertha and Bee. They lost no time at all in informing me that if I insisted on marrying a Catholic and in a Catholic church I would be out of their wills on the spot. Since it came as a great surprise to me that I was ever in them, my expectations of becoming an heiress were short-lived.

The three Bs overcame their prejudices sufficiently to attend the ceremony, but their curiously distinct observations remained less than tolerant.

My mother, who shared their suspicions, but to a quieter degree, went armed with a conspicuously large Methodist hymnbook which she wielded like a talisman.

Richard's brother-in-law, Jack Donnelly, a devout Catholic, was desperately trying to protect our everlasting souls from the other side. But his valiant bid to have a Mass said immediately after the ceremony was turned down by a Jesuit priest from Farm Street.

Religion, however, was not the only rift between our disparate families.

I come from a family of teetotalers. My maternal grandfather, Walter Wills, was uncompromisingly against the demon drink. His own father had been a very heavy drinker—a professional, grandfather Wills called him—and he had seen the misery and suffering it caused his mother. This one subject apart, my grandfather was the most lovable, gentle and understanding man I have ever met. He loved his wife Emily deeply. They behaved like a courting couple until the end of their days. He was rather dashing, slightly built—dapper, I suppose—and fancied himself immensely as a dancer. My grandmother was slim with pretty white curly hair. He was always tickling her—and anyone else who came within range. When he was eighty-five, and Emily wasn't much less than that, she would call out, "Come up to bed, lover, it's getting late." She was always rushing off to buy a new frock to wear for Walter. Every morning before he left for the office, she would go into the garden and pick a rose for his buttonhole. When he was Lord Mayor of Cardiff, the City Hall may have remained remarkably dry but it was always lively. He was a Liberal, of course, but politics took a secondary place in his life.

He had not permitted alcohol of any kind to be served at my parents' wedding. He would certainly not have approved of his son-in-law and granddaughter breathing fumes of brandy down the aisle. My father, who rarely imbibes, had suggested a stiff one each before we set off for the church that Saturday morning. Richard noted the brandy on my breath with some surprise—and a touch of

envy. He had spent the entire morning in pursuit of paja-
mas in Piccadilly—a hunt ordained by his family on dis-
covering he possessed none. Our reception, held at the
House of Lords, was attended by three hundred guests. It
had a distinct air of the United Nations about it. My father, in his time, had been Parliamentary Under-Secretary of State of the Colonies as well as Parliamentary
Under-Secretary of State for Commonwealth Relations.
Naturally, a great many of his political friends were there.
None of the stars of *A View from the Bridge* came, although all of the cast were invited. I simply did not
understand in those days that the class system in the
British theater was very rigid. Richard's position in the
play simply did not warrant their presence.

I wore a cream satin-and-lace Victorian wedding dress
and train that my Great-aunt Rhoda had been married in.
Great-aunt Rhoda was quite the best character the family
possessed. Her style had changed not a bit since the day
she wed Uncle Harry in 1894. The only known concession
she had ever made to changing fashion was the discreet
insertion of zips into her high button boots. A concession
that was noted but considered too delicate to be mentioned in her presence.

However, Great-aunt Rhoda was the closest the family
had ever come to the theatrical profession. She ran what
looked to all of us (and to the stage doorkeeper of the
Prince of Wales Theatre in Cardiff) something suspiciously like a theatrical boardinghouse. The suspicion was
always firmly discounted by Great-aunt Rhoda. If some of
her guests, she explained with an innocence that didn't
quite match her eyes, if some of her guests wanted to
show their appreciation each Friday morning with a little
something, it would be churlish of her to say no. However, once the little something was in her little hand it

stayed there. She did not altogether trust banks; the international monetary system, she hinted with an air of absolute but mysterious authority, had certain flaws. She preferred to keep her money in a safer place; this was understood to be beneath her mattress. Whether this was so or not, Great-aunt Rhoda maintained a twenty-four-hour vigil in her household, a prudence that ensured a noticeable impermanence about her staff.

Great-aunt Rhoda was a good cook. She had baked our wedding cake, which she now proudly stood guard over in the Lords dining room. The champagne was flowing almost but not quite as abundantly as some of the chieftains' robes. The millinery of Bridgend mixed quaintly with the more exotic finery of Bechuanaland. Great-aunts Bess, Bertha and Bee sat in a stately row observing the scene minutely.

I introduced Richard to them. I complimented them on their turnout, and remarked especially how pretty Great-aunt Bertha's hair was arranged. She smiled and thanked me. "I'll let you into a little secret," she said. "This is not my own hair. Well, it is mine because I paid for it. But I didn't grow it."

It was an extraordinarily mixed affair. Among my parents' guests, the Earl and Countess of Longford (then they were Lord and Lady Pakenham) appeared to be satisfied with the match. Lady Longford had presented me at Court and had taken an interest in my progress. A campaigning Catholic, Lord Longford suggested hopefully that I might now be a candidate for conversion to Rome. My father's response was less than enthusiastic. "My daughter's spiritual immortality concerns me rather less at this moment than the question of her daily bread," he said grimly.

I suppose he would have been even more alarmed had

he known that the sum total of the groom's fortune was £25.

But it was so easy on that day, in those magnificent historic surroundings, to put aside thoughts of mundane practicalities. The solemn splendid grandeur of that place could not be disturbed even by our religiously opposed families. The deep red carpets muffled any discordant sounds; the exquisite eighteenth-century Brussels tapestries, depicting the Triumph of the Gods and Episodes in the Life of Bathsheba, provoked no one. Fortunately, the Irish contingent was not aroused by the Tudor Roses that appeared to be carved everywhere: the flavor of the Tudors was strong to my brothers and me. Our parents, so very Welsh, had constantly emphasized our heritage.

After the toasts, Richard and I went to change. The Lord Chancellor, Lord Killmuir, had kindly allowed us to use his apartment. Lord Killmuir was married to Sylvia, sister of Rex Harrison.

Richard and I drove off in great style in a hired Rolls. We went straight to the Comedy Theatre, where Richard had two shows to do. I spent my wedding evening backstage in a broom closet of a dressing room Richard was sharing with Norman Mitchell.

That night we stayed at the Stafford, a small discreet hotel in St. James's. Richard had romantically but recklessly ordered champagne on ice to be waiting for us, and all sorts of lovely things to eat. The following morning, after a magnificent breakfast, a single thought occurred to us at exactly the same time: money.

All we had was the £25 that Richard's father (who had been unable to attend the wedding) had given him for the honeymoon. Even in 1957, £25 did not last very long in a Mayfair hotel when you were ordering champagne in your suite.

Richard sent for the bill at once. We realized that if we left immmediately, with a modicum of fuss and rather less than the minimum of tips, we would just have enough to take a taxi back to our bed-sitting room in Paddington.

It was a large, cheerful, bright room, which we liked— even if it was somewhat encumbered from the outside by an inordinate number of dustbins.

A *View from the Bridge* finally closed. With Richard out of work again, we couldn't afford to keep the Paddington apartment on. I managed to get a job in Blackpool—back in the old twice-nightly rep routine. Only now —with my Warrington experience behind me—I commanded a salary of £9 a week. Homeless again, Richard went to stay with my parents in Queens Gate. After a few weeks, he landed a small role in a modern-dress production of *Macbeth* at Stratford East. Rehearsal pay was £4 a week.

Whenever he was free for a few days, Richard would join me in Blackpool. Food, I remember, was always our main preoccupation. Probably because there was so little of it. We spent much of our free time searching for cheap places in which to eat. Our most riveting reading matter in those days was the menus stuck on steamy windows; we would only patronize those establishments which announced: "All Above Prices Include B & B [bread and butter] and Cup of Tea."

Having ordered our poached egg on toast or sometimes spaghetti on toast, we would settle down to our favorite game—where would we dine and what would we order the day money became no object? My idea of the ultimate meal then was to have a large steak in the Corrillo coffee bar on the Earls Court Road.

Payday was Friday. On Thursday, the manager could usually be persuaded to advance me five shillings. I gave

1/9*d* to Richard to go to the cinema; the rest of the money would go on our evening meal. It is difficult to write accurately about those times because, long-ago poverty, when you are poor no more, has a romantic distortion all of its own. It wasn't romantic at all, of course, although we were happy then. We laughed at our misfortunes, at the ridiculous hazards of hanging by a shoestring. Our finances were absurdly fragile. Dinner often depended on whether or not we could collect the sixpence deposit on a returned pie dish; with sixpence I could buy bacon scraps —and bacon and baked potatoes were always filling.

Richard went to Moscow with *Macbeth*. When he returned to London, my summer stint in Blackpool had come to an end. Together again, we were out of work and homeless.

We returned to bed-sitter land. We found an adequate room off the Earls Court Road with one dangerously smelly gas ring and a bathroom we had to share with about nine people.

It wasn't the sense of squalor that depressed me, but the thought that we were getting nowhere. I remembered as a child my mother's sister, Aunt Iris, comforting me over some heartbreak and telling me to welcome adversity as a challenge. It was, she said, from the difficult moments in life that one's character was formed. Certainly Richard and I were closer in those difficult days. We thought of each other's needs. Sharing when we had so little was easier than in the affluent days to come. Food was no more abundant in London than it had been in Blackpool. Michael and Sheila Van Bloeman, who had provided Richard with that amazing first dinner he gave me at Nevern Place, were exceptionally kind to us. Their casual but large-hearted dinner invitations always came at just the right moment.

The Troubadour was really an extension of their home. It was a vibrant place, full of young people with ideas and determination. Ken Russell put together one of his first films there, using the Troubadour regulars. Mort Sahl polished some of his best material there; and Marcel Marceau enthralled us night after night.

At this time, we were at the bottom of the spiral. I came into an inheritance from my parents of £150. My father suggested that I should invest it in an endowment policy to mature when I was fifty. I felt that if help wasn't a little more imminent, neither Richard nor I would make fifty. I decided to take the money.

I invested £100 in the fixtures and fittings of a five-year lease on a maisonette in the Earls Court Road.

The maisonette was above an underwear shop which catered entirely to the aging single lady of outsize proportions. The entrance to our apartment was at the side of a large bright display window wallowing in stupendous bloomers. Our visitors were obliged to stand as if gazing at all this intimate but bygone apparel while we descended two flights of stairs to admit them. My father spent many uncomfortable moments before that window. Enjoying his ordeal, Richard was always uncommonly slow in opening the door to him.

The stairs leading up to the first floor were narrow, dingy and uncarpeted. The wall was papered (many years before) in an unwelcoming sludge brown. The woodwork was painted dark brown and here and there were patches of what was once a gloss finish. On the first floor was a large, bleak L-shaped sitting room which we ignored, since we had no money to furnish it. On the second floor we had our bedroom. This contained a lovely old four-poster bed, a present from my grandparents, and an old green trunk, a present from my parents. The floorboards were bare and stained black, a dramatic effect somewhat upset by the skimpy blue-striped cotton curtains.

The kitchen was a tunnel; at the far end was the bathroom, secluded by a makeshift wall. The kitchen was well equipped: bone-china dinner service and hand-embroidered Irish table linen, Waterford crystal, Wedgwood coffee sets, gold-enameled teaspoons, silver napkin rings. We did very well with our wedding presents.

Despite these riches, our immediate needs were pressing. Richard was getting £6 10s. a week at Stratford East. But of this he had to pay 30s. a week in train fares and our rent was £6 a week. Even I could spot that this left us a bit short. Since nobody seemed to be getting hurt in the rush for my services, the only course left to us was to take in lodgers. I charged £4 a week for the top-floor double bedroom, and £2 a week for the single room.

I soon discovered the secret of being a successful landlady. When a potential lodger came to view, I moved in all the best pieces of furniture, bric-a-brac and finery I could lay my hands on. Once the room was taken, and the deposit paid, I would smartly shift half the stuff out again. It was a slightly dubious way of doing business, but very effective. The meager look the room had taken on between deposit and occupation usually caused consternation; I managed to avoid direct discussion of the matter by becoming violently preoccupied the moment I noticed that look of suspicion forming on the tenant's face.

Richard's landladies ("to a man," he said) had made all sorts of house rules. He preferred a more laissez-faire policy, except for one very rigid rule: the door was never to be opened before the identity and affiliation of the caller was ascertained. Visitors had to be thoroughly inspected from the third-floor front. On no account were we at home to men in dark blue mackintoshes; men in dark blue mackintoshes cut off electricity, disconnected your gas and read meters. Some were even bailiffs.

They were difficult, funny days, those early days above the underwear shop. Richard's strength seemed to grow amid the adversity. Although, for him, the life now was far the most comfortable and stable that he had led since his arrival from Ireland. Mine was a modest contribution perhaps, but I was still only a fledgling homemaker.

Rehearsing at Stratford East with the Joan Littlewood company, unable to stand his round in the local pub, he would scrupulously disappear at mealtimes.

Our regular diet continued to revolve around bacon scraps—enlivened from time to time with Beluga caviar which Richard had thoughtfully brought back from Russia. We possessed neither table nor chairs. We ate off our tin trunk. Such informality (which alarmed my brother Morgan, who came to dine with us the evening he returned from serving with the Welsh Regiment in Cyprus) had its advantages. Housework was minimal; one could spend only a limited amount of time polishing a tin trunk.

As a landlady I was not a total success. I was never immensely clever at summing up new lodgers. Some of them had charming smiles and tidy ways but were very bad pennies indeed. One very sweet-looking man ran off with a lot of our wedding presents early one morning. Richard caught him going out the door and gave chase. Passers-by were probably bemused by the sight of this large, tough-looking red-haired Irishman haring down the Earls Court Road shouting, "Stop thief! Stop thief! That man has got my pots and pans!" That anguished cry, that whole performance, was too theatrical to summon assistance and the thief got away.

We were never short of lodgers. One thing about being married to an Irishman, things happen. Like other Irishmen. I would never know, on waking in the morning, who was in the house. This could be alarming, especially if Richard had left early for rehearsals and forgotten to tell me how many people he had invited home the night before from the local. Richard had an unnerving propensity for inviting homeless strangers to stay the night: our empty sitting room on the first floor began to have a life of its own. I loved the carefree hospitable atmosphere of his parents' home in Limerick, but somehow I felt he might be carrying it to extremes in Earls Court.

A bedraggled line of bleary-eyed strangers queuing up for the only bathroom every morning tended to make me very fed up. Their unerring politeness, their anxiety not to be a nuisance, made me feel churlish. Moreover, some of the personal habits of these fleeting acquaintances left a lot to be desired. As I had a strictly limited household staff (me), I found this irksome. I was beginning to feel oppressed. Richard needed his times of solitude, but other people's privacy wasn't very high on his list of priorities.

Despite the volatile sense of uncertainty surrounding our domestic progress, Richard's career seemed to be moving slowly but unmistakably ahead. He had survived two seasons with the Theatre Workshop. A setup which had started with a band of actors and a director, Joan Littlewood, dedicated to bringing the theater to the man in the street, whether he wanted it or not. The actors, among them Harry Corbett, Jimmy Booth, Maxwell Shaw, Yootha Joyce, Brian Murphy and Avis Bunnage, often worked for well below Equity minimum, trying out new plays by such writers as Brendan Behan and Shelagh Delaney, always trying new ways of using the stage. The

Theatre Workshop Company became very fashionable, with West End audiences traveling adventurously to the East, where the theater was situated in Stratford East. Later their success was such that they had several plays running the West End simultaneously. Success is a giddy sensation, as we would discover ourselves. It is difficult to anticipate one's response to theatrical fame and the money it brings. Joan Littlewood succumbed gently. She took naturally to the delights of West End living.

Richard had also survived innumerable clashes with Miss Littlewood: I was told that he settled one contretemps by emptying a bag of cement over her head. The night she told him he was going to star in Pirandello's *Man, Beast and Virtue,* he came home in a state of complete shock. The play was to be directed by the distinguished Czech director Franz Yamnick. (Littlewood was going to Czechoslovakia on an exchange deal.) Richard had to read for Yamnick the next day.

When he read through the play that night he became convinced that Joan Littlewood had made a mistake. There were two male roles: a neurotic teacher, the leading pivotal character, and, a much smaller role, a rugged sea captain. "She means me to play the captain," Richard said. He spent most of the night reading the smaller part. By the morning he was word perfect and his fear of having to read for Yamnick was over. But Littlewood hadn't made a mistake at all. At the reading that morning, two actors began to deliver the captain's lines together. Richard was finally persuaded to read the other part; Yamnick was perceptive enough to let him play the teacher.

The rehearsal pay was as abysmal as always. I was now making fairly regular trips to the pawn shop. This was a new experience for me and my Welsh Baptist upbringing rebelled a bit. I would try to slink in and out of the pawn shop sideways, dressed in a mackintosh regardless of the weather. I felt that a mackintosh made me somehow less visible. The jewelry I was trying to hock was of no great value. I remember some pretty little brooches, bracelets, earrings, nine-carat rings, amethysts and garnets. Most of it was very old, but I never stopped to think how they had been loved and cherished in their time as I haggled over them for maybe just £5. Maybe that £5 would not give me anything like the pleasure those trinkets had given their previous owners down the years, but it would buy us a few of the necessities and that is what mattered most.

4. Taking Off

There is always one part in an actor's career, if he is lucky, however small, however insignificant that part may be, that opens the door. For Richard it was a role in a television play that turned the key.

The Pirandello play opened at Stratford East. The good reviews quickly got it transferred to the Lyric, Hammersmith. On the last night of the run a TV director called Cliff Owen was passing the theater and saw Richard's good notices on the billboards. He was looking for an Irish actor to play a blind man in *The Iron Harp*. He slipped into the theater and saw the last twenty-five minutes of *Man, Beast and Virtue*.

The following afternoon Richard got a call telling him to be at Cliff Owen's office in Soho at four o'clock sharp. The office had had some difficulty in finding Richard and it was now ten minutes to four. His only chance of making the appointment was to take a taxi, which would cost ten shillings. We broke open the gas meter. Richard got to Cliff Owen's office with minutes to spare.

He was kept waiting for an hour. Finally the secretary

told him to go home, as the part had been cast. This was too much for Richard. He pushed past the astonished girl and burst into Owen's office.

Cliff Owen is a large man and not one easily intimidated by anyone. Richard was livid. "Listen to me," he said. "I've broke my bloody neck getting here, I've robbed my gas meter of ten shillings for the taxi money. That's not only a criminal offense, it's bloody well two days' food for me and my wife. Now like it or not, you're going to hear me read for the fucking part."

Owen handed him the script.

"Go on," he said. "Let's hear you read."

Richard must have given the only good reading of his career. At the end of it Cliff Owen said, "You've got the part, Mr. Harris." The fee was £50.

A dear man, Robert Lennard, was in his bath when his wife called out, telling him to come and see an extraordinary young actor on television. Grumbling, wet, wrapped in a towel, he watched the young man's performance to the last line.

The morning after *The Iron Harp* was on television, Richard had an appointment with the agent Jimmy Fraser. He didn't have an agent and was trying to persuade Fraser, a man with a reputation for developing young talent, to take him on. Richard felt he wasn't making much of an impression at all when they were interrupted by a telephone call.

"Did you see a young actor called Richard Harris on television last night, Jimmy?" Bob Lennard asked.

"I did."

"He was very interesting," said Lennard. "Do you know who represents him?"

"I do," said Fraser without turning a hair.

"Let's meet," said Lennard.

"What did you have in mind?" Fraser asked.

"A seven-year contract," said Lennard.

"I'm not sure that we'd be interested in anything like that," said Fraser, slipping quietly into the plural. "But certainly let's talk."

Fraser put down the telephone and offered Richard his hand.

"So that's settled," he said.

In the middle of all this, I was summoned to the same ABPC studio to screen test for a role in a new movie; there was also talk of a long-term contract! Our luck seemed to be changing. Although I quickly realized after a day at Elstree Studios, being given the onceover by the experts, that Richard's chances of clinching a deal were perhaps greater than mine. Lighting cameramen, directors, make-up people, all seemed to be agreed on one thing: they were not happy with the way I looked. "Perhaps," somebody suggested, peering at me through half-closed eyes. "Perhaps we could bring her hairline forward. Her forehead is the real problem, don't you think? Much too large."

While I was waiting for the results of the screen test, tests of a more personal nature confirmed that I was pregnant. A few days later, without this pre-natal information to influence their decision, the studio informed me that I was not what they were looking for; my forehead was not the only thing that lacked star quality. A young actress named Mary Peach got the role.

I was disappointed, but the blow was considerably softened by the knowledge that I was to have a baby. Richard and I were apprehensive—and a little afraid, too. We had no real suspicion that we lacked some qualities considered useful in parenthood.

Now I suspect that Richard would never have signed that ABPC contract in 1958 if a baby was not due that August. It was the first and only time in his life that he succumbed to a regular pay packet.

Richard was beginning to spread his wings; he was growing in confidence. Even before the ABPC contract started he was building a colorful aura around himself. Even then hangers-on were beginning to collect around him. Money was still tight and sometimes desperately so, but that didn't inhibit Richard's excesses. There always seemed to be so many people to feed, so many evenings that stretched into days. People loved to listen to Richard's stories, his beguiling lies and often unbelievable truths; there were so many arguments, so many tears, so many songs. And always the Irish, talking about places and times and people I didn't understand and didn't know. I was beginning to feel out of it. The early excitement of sharing with Richard was going; the casual atmosphere that I had admired and encouraged was getting out of hand. A subtle change had taken place from our gypsying-around days. Now Richard was the master of the house and wanted no equal.

When we had been living in one room together it was difficult to play the host and hostess; our entertaining took place in local coffee bars or pubs. We had no responsibility beyond our weekly rent. Now it was different. We could invite people to our home, we could entertain, albeit in a casual style. Richard's overbearing personality became suffocatingly apparent. It was his friends' and his way of life that predominated.

A certain wildness seemed to be growing around us. It was a threatening wildness. It was ominous. There was never a moment of silence in that flat now. But more than that, there was never a moment, day or night, when Richard and I could be alone together.

I was feeling sick, fat and very lonely. I had lost touch with most of my old friends; my parents were on an official visit to Africa, my elder brother, Gwilym, was banking in Bangkok and Morgan had returned to Cyprus. The London I once knew seemed to be a million miles away from the life I was now leading. I could take the poverty, but this lack of privacy was beginning to destroy me. I had become an outsider in my own home. I felt very sorry for myself but quite unable to do anything about it. I felt that the encroaching threat of domesticity mortified Richard. I think it almost shamed him. He was determined not to appear trapped in any way. He would go to great lengths to demonstrate how undomesticated he was and how little control I had over him. If at the end of an evening in a pub, friends declined to return to our flat because of the lateness of the hour, Richard would become incensed. The slightest show of reluctance to accompany him ensured that the invitation would be pressed in such a way that further hesitation would have been pointless. I never knew whether this initial lack of enthusiasm to return with Richard was simply a clever ploy or genuine concern for my welfare, but it always ended the same way; if these people were genuinely concerned for me, I can only imagine they lacked genuine intelligence.

This made me very miserable. I was not a very amusing companion. My fits of depression were getting deeper and lasting longer. I didn't understand what was happening to me. My life had not prepared me for such melancholy; I had never had depressions before. Richard and I were growing further apart every day. We didn't have anything to say to each other. Gone were the intimate hours we had spent confessing our hopes and our fears. The days of lying in each other's arms content and wanting only each other's company. He began to look and to sound unfamiliar to me. There were moments when it all became so overpowering that I felt like giving up and one moment in particular when I thought that was the only answer. It is strange how casually we can treat life when the mind is so utterly exhausted and tormented. I went into the bathroom. I picked up a razor blade. I slashed my left wrist. I passed out. I never could stand the sight of blood. Richard's reaction to my desperation demonstrated clearly to me how very far apart we had moved. He was totally unaware of my loneliness. I felt I had moved to the very periphery of his life.

I came to in St. Stephen's Hospital. He was beside me. In those days attempted suicide was a criminal offense. Richard had loyally explained to the doctors that I had slipped while cutting linoleum. Later he berated me for embarrassing his friends! We never spoke of it again.

We were overspending. I was getting very large. I had no maternity clothes. Inspired by Scarlett O'Hara, I went to my parents' home (they were still in Africa) and carefully examined the curtains. I decided against the blue velvet in the dining room and settled for the more modest blue serge in the maid's room. These I made into what I thought was a passable maternity outfit. I had no qualms about wearing it to a rather smart occasion at the Royal Festival Hall. Richard, having just signed the ABPC contract, had been invited to make up a table of television personalities. We extravagantly took a table for ten. During the evening—we had behaved fairly well—somebody broke a glass. When Richard got the bill at the end of the evening, we had been charged for ten glasses. Richard pointed out the discrepancy. The headwaiter—irritatingly aloof—declined to discuss the matter at all. I said, very well, if we were to be charged for ten glasses we still had nine to go. I saw a look of disbelief as I stood up in all my pregnant regalia and solemnly and very slowly dropped nine glasses to the floor. Unfortunately, the management failed to appreciate the simple logic of my performance. As we left the Hall the police were there. Richard is not a man for evasive action in such situations. He simply put his head down and charged his way into about fourteen astonished constables . . . and a plate-glass window. We finished the evening at St. George's Hospital Casualty Department, where Richard had a dozen stitches put in a nasty cut on his hand. However, the evening ended uneventfully.

A few days later I attended my parents' official homecoming at Victoria Station. Once again I wore my curtain outfit. I noticed a few puzzled glances from my mother; clearly the blue serge struck a half-familiar chord. Fortunately, we were quickly swept up in an exchange of hugs and hellos. Later she took me to one side to tell me that she didn't think I looked terribly well turned out and advised me to try for something a little better tailored and more concealing.

Until that moment, Richard had not given my wardrobe a thought. He was horrified when he realized that I was dressed in the maid's curtains. He got some money from somewhere and rushed me off to Harrods, where he insisted on buying me several glamorous but quite impractical outfits in white. I loved them; I felt feminine again.

Richard went to Scotland to begin work on his first film. It was called *Alive and Kicking* and starred Sybil Thorndike. I did not go with him; the baby was due at any moment.

Due to the fact that I was two weeks overdue, the

proud father was able to be present at the birth. He was allowed into the labor ward. I was a National Health patient and found myself helped and encouraged by an inordinate number of students. I felt well looked after with plenty of gas and air and soothing voices. Richard held my hand. The ward seemed to be full of women on the point of delivery and the shrieks and groans were rather plentiful. Suddenly I was alone. The students, the nurses, Richard had all disappeared. There seemed to be an emergency of some kind behind the screens that had now been placed around my bed.

Richard had fainted.

The entire nursing staff were engaged in reviving him, telling him he would be all right, to take it easy, to stay calm.

He was prescribed a stiff drink to be taken off the premises at frequent intervals. This shrewd medical advice met with his approval. The patient began to make a steady and splendid recovery.

Damian's birth was easy and uncomplicated. When finally mother and child were left on their own for a moment we regarded each other—or at least I regarded him —in total wonderment. Our solitude was soon interrupted by Richard. He had made a most remarkable recovery in the Rose and Crown.

Richard had not slept all night. He just sat and stared and stared at his son. When he was finally persuaded to pick him up, they both looked so vulnerable: one so tiny and helpless, the other so large and tender.

When Damian was six weeks old, we all went to Dublin. Richard was doing a film with James Cagney. One of the greatest Hollywood actors, Cagney one day did his famous dance routine from *Yankee Doodle Dandy* for us. We both realized it was close to the end of an era.

Shake Hands with the Devil was one of Cagney's last films; he announced his retirement shortly after the picture was finished.

Although it was not a good picture, Richard came out of it okay and was quickly offered another picture by the director Michael Anderson. The picture was *The Wreck of the Mary Deare*, starring Gary Cooper, to be made in Hollywood.

The night before our departure for Los Angeles, we were to be my father's guests at the London Welsh Ball at the Royal Festival Hall. After our last experience at the Festival Hall we were not especially keen to return, and I'm sure the management entertained similar feelings. Since my father was the president of the London Welsh Society, any question of us being actually banned from the Hall was clearly a ticklish one. The management could only hope for the best. The hope was in vain. Sian Phillips, the Welsh actress, was among the guests of honor; she was escorted by her fiancé, Peter O'Toole. O'Toole was a brilliant young actor with a clear destiny. We had been students together at RADA. He was lean, handsome and possessed a challenging humor.

Perhaps it was the sight of so many Welshmen gathered together that inspired and challenged Ireland's Harris and O'Toole to exert their presence. Their impromptu cabaret performance did not go down particularly well. Disgusted members of the London Welsh Society were arriving at my father's table and resigning on the spot. It was very awkward for him. We were finally escorted from the building, Sian Phillips, O'Toole, Harris and me, never to be welcomed again.

I was glad that our departure for the States was very early the next morning, before my parents had a chance to contact me.

We arrived in Hollywood exhausted. We had taken forty-eight hours to fly there over the Pole. We were in a turboprop airliner and one of the engines had caught fire over North Dakota. The pilot announced our predicament. After dumping all our fuel, we landed safely. We changed planes and continued our journey.

We had been flying for about an hour when the pilot announced that another engine had caught fire. We went through the same emergency procedure in Salt Lake City.

I realized for some time now that Richard would not in many circles be immediately recognized as a devout Catholic. I had come to think of him more as a bargaining Catholic. I never saw him bargain with anyone harder and faster than he did with the Almighty during those hours.

He thought of Damian. Richard vowed then that never again would he and I fly in the same plane. And we never did again.

We drove straight from L.A. Airport to MGM Studios in Culver City. Hollywood! It was just as I had imagined. There was a genuine sense of history, yet everything seemed so new and so impermanent. One thought of Chaplin and Pickford, Garbo, the Gish sisters, Gable, Fairbanks. But now there were the wide vast freeways and trailer parks, used-car lots and the sprawling repetitious sense of suburbia. The bright sharp sunshine was lovely, but it also revealed all the shoddiness of temporary glamour. But the sense of excitement at MGM was real enough. One could feel the urgency.

We were booked into a motel not far from the studios. It seemed immensely glamorous. The rooms were built around a large sunlit pool and the permanently midnight-dark bars and restaurants seemed very sophisticated to me.

The realization that our social life was not exactly top drawer was gradual; our lack of mobility seemed at first to be our only serious deprivation. I had not passed my driving test and Richard had had his license taken away for life in Ireland. This, on reflection, was quite a remarkable feat, since the Highway Code is not the most zealously observed piece of legislation in Limerick. However, they couldn't overlook the fact that Richard had managed to drive his car into a Corporation bus. Twice.

We knew no one in Beverly Hills and no one at the studios made any moves to know us. We spent all our spare time wandering around downtown Hollywood, looking at the people and the sights and going to the movies; it was not unlike the way Richard spent his days waiting for me in Blackpool, only now there was sunshine. We still didn't have much money, but at least enough to get by.

I still didn't realized the blunder we had made. But Richard was certainly beginning to realize it, although he never spoke about it to me. (Perhaps our closeness had already been irreparably damaged, although that was something else I didn't realize then). He recognized that Hollywood is entered by many doors and an actor is judged by and often confined to his place of entry. It was a baffling, barbed game and we didn't know the rules. And worse than that, there was nobody there to teach us. We didn't even know the right restaurants to get the wrong table in.

Richard's pride was hurt; his colossal ego was put to the test. I didn't understand then that his sudden violence followed by the now familiar long sullen withdrawals was more likely caused by anger at himself for being caught in that position than by any cooling of his love for me. I know now that you have to decide early in life which way it will be: you either call the tune or dance to someone else's pipes.

The hard sell was something new to me. I was certainly taken in. It was weeks before I realized that our glamorous motel wasn't glamorous at all but slightly seedy and very much on the wrong side of town. Professionally, Richard was up against the wall. His billing on the movie was lowly and his contract protected him barely at all.

I felt lonely and homesick and missed Damian. Richard was every bit as lonely and even more frustrated, especially since he seemed unable to talk to me about all the things that were dawning on him. It was the beginning of Richard's professional growing up. I understood none of this. I saw a side of Hollywood I would never see again. We were on the outside looking in.

Gary Cooper became gravely ill during the making of that picture. Although we didn't know it then, he was, in fact, dying of cancer. His wife and daughter came to the set almost every day, watching him play some very rigorous and intensely uncomfortable scenes. The studio had built half of the ship, the *Mary Deare,* in a big tank. The same tank had been used in the Esther Williams movies. Cooper was often submerged in the water in the tank for a considerable time. He never missed a day although it was obvious he was suffering very much. I couldn't help thinking what an extraordinary life the film world is. A man right up to his death will go on playing makebelieve. And it wasn't even a very good picture in the end.

The fights which had long been a feature of our marriage were getting pretty rough. Richard has a very direct and sometimes painful way of showing his displeasure. One was never left in any doubt about his feelings. I was very relieved when it was decided I should go home ahead of him, sailing from New York on the *Queen Elizabeth*.

On the boat I had fun. For the first time in what seemed like years I felt young again. I felt almost free. On that trip I met a charming RAF officer. The attraction was mutual and apparent. He was very attentive and we spent a great deal of time together. Unfortunately, I was far too afraid that I would not be able to lie to Richard convincingly and my shipboard romance remained boringly platonic. The really irritating thing about it was that Richard didn't believe me anyway. I might just as well have enjoyed a romance. Even so, it was a memorable crossing. I fell totally and naturally into old familiar ways; days took on remembered shapes and recognizable patterns. I enjoyed again the evening drink parties and changing for dinner. I felt fussed over and attractive. And I enjoyed having to rely upon myself once more. I suppose many women who marry young and have children quickly have gone through a similar experience, a reawakening. During that Atlantic crossing I realized that my life had not only changed, it had practically stopped. I'd stopped reading books, stopped listening to other people's views, stopped developing as a person. There seemed to have been so little time for introspection, for ideas, for curiosity. I got used to listening to the comments and criticisms made by Richard; it was so much easier to repeat his views than to form and express my own. It is a fatal trap, so easy to fall into. A husband cannot be entirely to blame if he needs to find more stimulating company elsewhere.

I had come to depend on Richard's personality so much that I hesitated before accepting invitations to the many parties on board. I felt shy and inadequate on entering a roomful of strangers.

The young officers were most gallant, of course, and I

enjoyed again the sensation of not being contradicted by young men while making the most inaccurate and sweeping statements.

The five days at sea were soon over. As I sat nursing a large brandy on the boat train, I began to feel nervous. What would be waiting for me in London? There had been a decided strain in our relationship when I left Los Angeles. I no longer felt at ease with Richard. I didn't like to think of it as fear . . . more a certain wariness, perhaps.

5. Beyond Our Means

After a few fretful querulous days in London that did nothing to heal our growing sense of separateness, Richard left to make a picture in Ireland. It was a good role —Robert Mitchum's fanatical IRA sidekick—in a bad movie called *A Terrible Beauty*. Our quarrels continued on the telephone for several days. I hated telephone arguments. I decided to pay a surprise visit to Ireland.

Sitting in the pretty (but rather uncomfortable) Victorian steam train which meandered south along the coastline from Dublin to Bray, I felt again the same nagging apprehension I had felt on the boat train a week before. In the distance the Dublin mountains lie in a gentle blue mist. The serenity of the setting seemed only to increase my nervousness. I felt more and more as if I were going to meet a stranger. I simply didn't know any more what Richard felt about us, about our relationship, our future. They were matters we never discussed any more— although Richard still insisted he could discuss anything. Only he could never differentiate between a discussion and an argument. Even in the friendliest discussion he had to keep score. His scoring system was mysterious and seemed consistent only in its favorable bias toward him. His idea of a constructive discussion entailed much jumping up and down, a great deal of physical emphasis, often culminating in hugs and kisses—if he'd made a particularly brilliant point (in his opinion)—and even loud and prolonged applause for his own performance. I found this distracting. I usually lost my train of thought amid the self-congratulatory turmoil.

As I neared the little seaside town of Bray, I was beginning to wish I had never left London. I had no idea what his reaction to my visit would be.

When I arrived at the hotel, a former country house, a short distance from Bray, everyone was still at the studio. I needed a drink but decided against it. I had to be calm and collected: one needed all one's faculties unimpaired to confront Richard. The minutes passed slowly. The quiet was finally shattered by the sound of dozens of vehicles—cars, vans, buses—coming up the gravel driveway together. There was a lot of shouting and banging of doors, a great deal of ragging and laughter. You can tell a lot about how a film is going from the way in which the cast and crew return to the hotel. I felt a surge of hope. They told Richard at the desk that I was waiting for him in his room. He came in looking serious but walked over to me and hugged me without a word.

"I'm pleased you've come, Lilliput," he said.

The picture was going well. Richard admired Robert Mitchum. He had never met such an open and generous actor as Mitchum. "Don't be taken in by that languorous style of his," Richard told me. "He doesn't miss a trick, that one." Mitchum was also very popular with the crew. It was a happy production and only Raymond Stross, the producer, seemed out of step; he was on nobody's popularity list.

Robert Mitchum and his wife, Dorothy, had rented a house close to the hotel. They invited us to dinner that evening. Bob did the cooking. He is a casual but excellent cook. The Mitchums were to become two of my dearest friends, but at that moment I just felt they were warm unassuming people. There was nothing "Hollywood" about them at all.

The combination of Bob and Richard did not make for coziness exactly. We spent many remarkable evenings in Dublin. One night we were dining at a small restaurant, a favorite theatrical haunt. Bob was always being asked for his autograph. This particular evening one man was being especially persistent and very insensitive. Time and again he came to our table and asked Bob to sign pieces of paper, rudely interrupting our conversation. Bob signed because he knew it is easier to sign than to refuse. Finally the man approached with yet another scrap of paper and imperiously told Bob, "Sign this. It's for my wife."

Bob didn't even look up. He wrote on the piece of paper pushed under his nose, continuing with our conversation. Within thirty seconds the man was back again, full of fury. He hit Bob across the face. A silence fell over the whole room. Bob simply went on with his story, not registering the blow at all. At last he looked at his unnerved assailant.

"Next time you do that, make sure you drop me good, or I'll break your motherfucking neck," he said quietly. The man was no longer in a mood to argue. He turned, collected his wife and left hurriedly. I was mystified by the whole business. Later I heard that Bob's last autograph read, "Up your ass. Kirk Douglas."

Strange as it may seem, Bob and Dorothy Mitchum

were a calming and helpful influence in our lives. They'd seen it all and been through the thick of it. They knew the score. Exactly.

Richard at that time was drinking very heavily in the evenings, never during the day and never on the set, but as long as he didn't touch brandy all would be more or less all right. Brandy had the most terrifying effect on him . . . and subsequently on me!

Nothing ever stood still for long with Richard. We could be fighting uncontrollably one hour and the next laughing and loving and full of hope for our future together. I always fell for his charm and his blarney. He could always make me believe that my fears and anxieties were ridiculous and unfounded. We left Ireland together full of confidence. I had been taken in again.

Richard opened in *The Ginger Man* at the Fortune Theatre in September 1959. The play was adapted by J. P. Donleavy from his own novel and directed by Philip Wiseman. It was a small production, the first managerial venture of designer Tony Walton, who was then married to Julie Andrews.

The play and Richard opened to admiring notices. Sebastian Dangerfield was a marvelous role by anybody's standards, and perfect for Richard. A bawdy, sponging law student, Dangerfield was a man of mad violent moods and wild Irish talk, drunk with poetry, big ideas and brandy; Richard played him to the hilt. Wendy Craig played his come-down-in-the-world wife, representing the English bourgeoisie, who finally has enough and leaves him, taking their baby with her. Isabel Dean played the plain, prudish spinster lodger whom Dangerfield seduces and humiliates. Ronald Fraser appeared as an aging university student haunted by poverty and his own persistent virginity.

The Ginger Man seemed set for a long run in the tiny Fortune Theatre. Had Richard left his performance on stage after the final curtain, all would have been well.

Unfortunately, somewhat obsessed by Stanislavski and all the talk of the Actors' Studio in New York at that time, Richard continued to live the grotesque Dangerfield off stage. Characters that he enjoyed playing, he assimilated into his own life, for the duration of the play or the film. This led to situations surpassing anything the producers were putting on stage each evening. Due to the location of the Fortune, in Covent Garden—where the pubs remain open outside the customary licensing hours—impromptu and prolonged parties happened often.

The most cautious estimate was that *The Ginger Man* would run for six months. This, together with Richard's regular income from ABPC, encouraged us to look for a more comfortable apartment. I eventually found a flat in Allen House, a block off Kensington High Street. The rent was £ 15 a week. We were again living way beyond our means. The one thing Richard and I had not lost in common was our tendency to spend whatever money we had. Living within our means had always been an arrangement neither of us cared for.

I felt the opulence of our new address an auspicious moment which merited a change in my appearance. After a visit to the hairdresser's I was a paler shade of my former self.

I arranged for the removal men to start early in the morning. I told them to leave our bedroom until last. Richard liked to sleep until at least midday to recuperate from his various performances the night before. When finally everything was packed into the removal van except our bedroom furniture, I led the way in, telling the removers to be as quiet as possible. Whether they saw it as a professional challenge or a huge joke, I don't know. They set about the task with quiet enthusiasm. Removing their shoes in the manner of worshippers entering an Eastern temple, they proceeded to dismantle the room around Richard. Finally all that remained was the four-poster bed—and its occupant.

"Don't wake him, lady," the foreman said. "He looks as if he needs all the beauty sleep he can get."

They removed the canopy. Then the posts. Now all that remained was the mattress and, of course, Richard. The removal men, by now thoroughly caught up in the enterprise, offered to take the mattress and Richard to the van. It was an appealing notion. At that moment he woke up. He accepted his position in the naked room. He told me to get a move on, we were entertaining Don Murray and his wife Hope Lange to lunch. This was news to me and to the ever-willing removal men. If we were going to be "at home" anywhere that day, the foreman said dryly, it would have to be in the back of his van. It had been a hard morning, he pointed out justly, and now they were off to lunch. We all ended up in the pub on the corner.

That evening, as I was still unpacking, Richard returned from the theater with J. P. Donleavy in tow. Donleavy, Richard informed me in a tone carelessly denying blame, would be spending the night with us. Our first night in our new apartment hardly saw me in the most hospitable mood; Donleavy did not bring out the most bountiful side of my nature at the best of times. He disturbed me. Not only did I dislike him, I distrusted him. I had the feeling that he enjoyed creating tricky situations just to see how one would cope, what sort of dialogue we would inflict on each other. I didn't relish the idea of turning up in one of his dramas. To feel oneself under the microscope is not a pleasant sensation; I didn't have too much confidence that I would come out of any Donleavy plot too triumphantly.

Perhaps I was being unduly sensitive at that time. Our marriage was going downhill rapidly. *The Ginger Man* had been running for about three weeks when I made the familiar "going home to mother" speech and exited, clutching Damian. (I was aware that even this scene seemed like an extension of the play.) My poor parents on this occasion had all three offspring arrive home unexpectedly within hours of each other. My father, a prudent and practical man, placed a collection box beside the telephone and told us we must all contribute. It was, he felt, going to be the night of the long calls.

My separation from Richard took on a more permanent look. I started divorce proceedings. My mother tried to mediate, but to no avail. Richard took a flat and Damian and I returned to Allen House. I was obliged once again to take in a lodger. Suddenly, to everyone's surprise, *The Ginger Man* folded. It had lasted just six weeks. Richard's disappointment was immense. He decided to take it to Dublin and it opened at the Gaiety Theatre in October 1959—and closed after three performances. The critic of the *Irish Independent* dismissed it in three paragraphs as "one of the most nauseating plays ever to appear on the Dublin stage." The Irish certainly know how to treat a dramatic entertainment that doesn't meet with their approval.

It was a bad time for Richard. His ambition to return to Ireland in triumph was dashed. It hit him harder than anyone imagined. He fought hard for that role. He was originally offered O'Keefe (the part eventually played by Ronald Fraser), with Jason Robards playing the Ginger Man. "You can't do that," he shouted at Donleavy. "I am the Ginger Man."

Almost immediately after this, Richard learned that his mother was dying of cancer. He went home to Limerick.

Only to Richard could she speak of her fears—not of death, she didn't have fear of that; she was a very religious woman with great spiritual strength—her fears for the family. She knew the weak links in it and wanted Richard to accept responsibility for them. Richard at first seemed an unlikely candidate for such a role. He and his mother had battled constantly, but he adored her and she saw in him a courage and spirit that had once been hers. I had grown to love her and was shocked to hear of her illness. She did not know of our plans for divorce and I immediately agreed to go to Ireland in case she suspected something was wrong between us. I stayed with Richard's sister Harmay. She was kind to me, and we got on well. At first we were distant and cool toward each other, Richard and I. As the days passed, our defenses were lowered; I admired the way he coped with the situation, the gentleness with which he cared for his mother. I would have to leave the room after only a few minutes, as did most people, because I couldn't stop the tears at the sight of this once strong, laughing, handsome woman reduced to a thin whisper, barely an indentation beneath the sheets.

Richard never left that room while she was awake; he sat day after day, holding her hand, chatting away, keeping everything around her as normal as possible.

I finally had to return to London. I had been back only a few hours when I got a call from Richard. His mother had died. I left at once for Dublin. I caught a milk train to Limerick, arriving early the next morning. Richard met me on a frosty deserted railway station. His eyes were so tired and lonely. I knew then that he had lost the person who had been dearest to him in the whole world.

He loved her dearly, he grieved silently. It was a remarkable relationship and I didn't begin to understand it until it had ended. I knew that the family would never be the same again.

It seemed as if the whole of Limerick turned out to pay their last respects. In spite of caring for her own family of nine children, she had found time to love and protect a considerable number of others.

Richard and I had been drawn together; I felt he needed me. I wanted so much to try again.

Richard was emotionally and physically spent. There was an emptiness in his eyes I had never seen there before. I knew he had to get away, to submerge himself in some self-forgetting activity. When his agent came up with a television play in New York with Eric Portman I urged him to take it. We parted at Shannon. I felt very low, perhaps because I knew there was nothing more I could do. Two weeks later I received a cable. "How about a honeymoon in Paris? Richard."

He had booked a suite at the Ritz. It was grand and beautifully old-fashioned. He was waiting for me in Le Bar au Ritz. There was champagne on ice. (God knows how he paid for it.) I saw at once that New York had been good for him. "Honeymoons, however late, should always be memorable," he said, pouring the wine.

That evening we had dinner at Maxim's. Ever since I had seen the film *Gigi* I had longed to have dinner at that restaurant. I imagined the glamorous crowd of beautiful international woman and handsome sophisticated men wafting in and out in the most superior manner. Everyone would be dressed extravagantly. Everyone would be amazingly witty. I wore a long white chiffon gown and Richard wore his new velvet dinner jacket.

Maxim's, alas, was not the gathering place of the international crowd that night. Indeed, only one other table in the entire room was occupied.

Richard was undeterred. He ordered champagne in a voice that suggested it was not the first and certainly would not be the last bottle of champagne he would order that night. On hearing his voice the bored and hitherto silent orchestra came to life. With a small polite smile in my direction, the orchestra leader led his ensemble into a lively rendition of "When Irish Eyes Are Smiling"!

In Paris we seemed to be enveloped by a sense of isolation and anonymity. We made love freely but the innocence had gone and we both knew it. A dream had been shattered. Although it was unreasonable to believe in that dream, we were both hurt by its going. We clung to each other hoping the ache would ease. It helped, but only time would ever dull the deeper hurt. Why is it that having an affair is more pleasurable than marital bliss? We recognized that we had allowed our sex life and pillow talk to become mechanical and mundane. "From now on," Richard told me that first time in Paris, "we shall have a series of beautiful affairs." We made a pact. Never again would we allow other people and problems to interrupt our reunions. After any separation we would always meet in a hotel room. We would stay at least two days and rediscover each other. We would not allow domesticity to intrude and inhibit our appetites.

For these reunions in hotel rooms, I would do my best to be strange and explorable, with new clothes and new ideas to excite him. He would fill the rooms with lilacs or lilac-colored flowers. He liked me dressed in lilac; it was his favorite color, although it did nothing for me. He called me Lilac Lil, except for a brief moment when he bought me a diamond and I became Diamond Lil.

I found hotel rooms erotic. I welcomed the anonymity and transitory feeling hotel rooms gave us. We became different characters, new personalities, for those few days of reconciliation. It gave a new excitement to our marriage, a new dimension.

On our return to London, Richard gave up his bachelor quarters and moved back into the flat and we resumed our life together. But now we had a new awareness of each other, perhaps even a new respect.

Death had always preoccupied Richard's thoughts much more than mine. I put this down to his Catholic education and upbringing. Catholics seemed to attach a disproportionate importance to death and dying; the Welsh, the nonconformists, always seemed to be more concerned with arrangements here than the arrangements in the hereafter. I felt that his obsession with his own demise was macabre; he would telephone me and, pretending to be a policeman, announce his death or near death in some accident or other. Old friends in Limerick had also received similar disturbing calls.

For some reason I was never able to ascertain, he also became convinced that all would be over for mankind (or an extraordinary number of it among his acquaintances) by A.D. 1965. He formed a club with a select and morbid membership of friends who shared his views.

They took it seriously—as, indeed, such a grave point of view should be taken seriously. The philosophy was commemorated in a club called simply but pertinently The 65 Club. Headed notepaper ("The 65 Club" in funereal Gothic) was printed and distributed to members, including Georgia Brown and Edna O'Brien. With a conceited sense of immortality, I declined to join their number. Not even as an associate member. I spent the early months of

1966 gleefully leaving the now offending notepaper in conspicuous places.

Although we were now more relaxed together, *The Ginger Man* continued to shadow our lives. Richard simply could not resist provoking my parents; in every interview he gave he managed to send them up. My mother and father are inclined to take newspaper reports seriously. My father, being a lawyer and politician, has a particularly cautious attitude toward the press. Richard's opinions of the House of Lords were among the many items he was offering for publication. "The House of Lords is just a rich man's labor exchange where the old boys sign on their three pounds a day" was a favorite line of his. "The only good thing about it is the grub. Steak and kidney pie for seven and sixpence isn't bad!" Apart from the perverse pleasure he got from these digs at my parents, he also collected a lot of publicity by reminding people of his titled connections. I still thought it was a pretty dubious way to acquire social stature. My father had a slightly better rapport with him than my mother managed to achieve. He did help Richard form his own company and for a while was its chairman. But any real understanding between them was unachievable; they were simply poles apart. My parents' life style, for example, was one of rigid routine: breakfast was unfailingly at 8 A.M. in the dining room; my brothers and I were expected to attend, whether we wanted breakfast or not. Days were planned weeks ahead.

Richard's career, unlike our haphazard life, continued to move forward. He was now working at Elstree on *The Long and the Short and the Tall*. It was his second film under the ABPC contract and he got billing under Laurence Harvey and Richard Todd. Larry was a generous, sophisticated man, with a self-deprecating wit. I never formed a clear impression of Richard Todd. He chose to remain apart from the other actors. I remember hearing that he now spent more time farming than he did acting.

The picture also starred Richard's old *Ginger Man* pal Ronnie Fraser. It was an all-male cast and they had an almost prep school enthusiasm for pranks. Only Richard Todd failed to fall in with the general mood.

One day Larry Harvey told me a marvelous story. He noticed that Todd was engaged in some surreptitious but industrious footwork on the set, a Malaysian jungle. Considerably shorter than Larry and Richard, Todd was building a mound on which to stand in the next scene.

As the picture progressed, Todd never seemed to achieve his extra inches. Indeed, some people on the set remarked that he seemed to be getting shorter. I don't know whether he ever discovered the truth—but beside his own carefully prepared mound would always be two larger ones.

Lunch became the social event of the day. Joined by John Ireland, a great friend of Larry's who was filming at a nearby studio, each actor in turn played host and each tried to outdo the other: Larry's own special Chablis would arrive, chilled, from London; Ronnie Fraser would surprise them with some rare delicacy acquired from unknown regions of Soho; Richard provided a rather splendid but mysterious fish lunch which Larry pronounced was shamrock salmon.

One evening this luncheon club met for dinner, together with their wives, at Alexander's in the Kings Road. Larry was married to Margaret Leighton. She looked marvelously chic, although, as somebody remarked, she wore her Paris fashions with an English accent. The spirit of the Elstree luncheon did not travel well, alas. There

was a definite tension in the air. It was the first time we
had met Maggie Leighton and her attitude toward us
was one of brittle condescension. The knives were out
between her and Larry and it was clear that their marriage was not exactly made in heaven. Larry was in the
middle of a story when Rex Harrison came over to our
table. He and Maggie talked quietly and exclusively to
each other for nearly ten minutes. Larry simply got on
with his story. When Rex finally kissed her cheek and left
she turned furiously on Larry. "For Christ's sake, Larry,
why can't you be polite to my friends? I have to suffer
your bloody friends."

Our friendship had only reached the superficial stage;
her remark suggested that that was where it would remain.

Rex Harrison, on the other hand, did not disappoint me
at all. He was exactly as I had imagined him: handsome,
elegant, worldly and so very English. He was also rather
frightening. He had an aloof quality about him that was
inhibiting. I had the feeling it was better not to speak at
all than to say something less than brilliant. Wrongly. He
is such a marvelous actor.

After *The Long and the Short and the Tall*, producer
Carl Foreman signed Richard for *The Guns of Navarone*.
It was a small role but MGM were impressed enough to
offer him the role of a mutineer in the epic remake of *Mu-
tiny on the Bounty*, with Marlon Brando and Trevor
Howard.

Richard was thrilled. When the script arrived the role
was so small he turned it down flat. Some weeks later, he
received a new script. His role had been enlarged and
made more interesting. Richard was learning fast. Our
trip to Hollywood had not been wasted after all. But
again Richard refused the role. They upped his fee. But

he was holding out for more than money. He thought this could be the big one—the one to bring him real stature. He took a deep breath and said no matter how much money they offered him, he would only play the role if he had equal billing to Marlon Brando. They said it was impossible: "Brando is Brando."

Richard said, "All right, I'll do it if I have equal billing to Trevor Howard."

They again said it was impossible: "Howard is better known than Harris."

Richard argued that he was as well known as Howard had been at his age!

The illogical effrontery of this argument made them think for a while. But they wouldn't give in. It was a battle of wits. Two days before Richard was due to leave for the location in Tahiti—if the studio gave in to his demands—I was due to leave for Manchester for a television play. He came with me to the station. As the train was pulling out he said, "See you here next week—or in Tahiti next month, Lilliput." The next day he telephoned me in Manchester. His voice was brimming with confidence. Before he told me the news I knew it would be Tahiti next month.

Richard always traveled light, usually with no more than a bottle of Bourbon in his hand. At London Airport, a stewardess greeted him, "Good morning, Mr. Harris." Richard's fame was still gathering: he was not used to being recognized in public.

"How do you know me?" he asked.

"I recognized you from your hand luggage," she said smartly.

Meanwhile, back in Manchester, I was rehearsing a play in which I had one line. Most actors have stories of how in the early days of their careers they hopelessly fluffed their only line in their first performance. I managed to do just that in my last performance. I loved the theater dearly. But passion is not enough without some talent. I knew as I traveled back from Manchester that I had given my farewell performance.

I was feeling wretched, and I looked awful. I tried to organize Damian, the nanny, a young Welsh girl, and our departure for the South Pacific. I was finding it hard going. I felt quite exhausted. I had no energy at all and friends were shocked at my appearance. I kept feeling faint and giddy. Surely, I thought, giving up the theater shouldn't have this effect on me?

Then I started being sick in the mornings. I was pregnant.

Tahiti was not among Dr. Spock's suggested resorts for young children and expectant mothers. When we arrived there I knew why. Jets were not flying to Tahiti then. The runway was too short. We arrived in a small plane of nostalgic vintage belonging to South Pacific Airways. It had been an eventful flight.

In New York, Damian was rushed to the Medical Center with a sudden high temperature which just as suddenly disappeared. We flew to San Francisco, then on to Honolulu, where we had a twelve-hour layover before the last leg to Tahiti.

In Tahiti we were asked to wait in our seats while the Health Officers came aboard and cheerfully sprayed us with a vile-smelling disinfectant. This salubrious ceremony puzzled me for a long time afterward, since it soon became apparent to me that no novel disease could possibly be introduced to that infected island.

I stumbled from the plane, choked by the disinfectant and blinded by the sun. Hula-hula girls, oblivious to my intense discomfort, decorated us with leis. Their perfume was extraordinarily strong and before I reached the small makeshift customs hall I felt horridly sick. I also started to itch most uncomfortably around the neck. Since I was carrying Damian in one arm and a folding Christmas tree in the other—it was Christmas Eve—I was in no position to scratch myself.

I was not at my best.

There was no Richard to meet us. No car, no one from the studios, and very soon simply no one.

Across the way from the ramshackle shed in which we now stood amid a customs-cleared sea of luggage and the unlikely folding Christmas tree, I noticed a barman in the process of putting up the shutters.

I explained our plight. He offered to contact his cousin who had a car. It was a start. The barman said his cousin would drive us to Papeete—the capital, chief port, and business center—where we would surely find somebody connected with the film. It sounded like a bit of a long shot to me but I really had no other choice.

There were no hotels in Papeete, the well-known capital, chief port, and business center. All the hotels, the barman's cousin explained, were built in other parts of the island. I had no idea where Richard might be. I had sent a cable, advising him of our arrival on December 24, via the MGM production office. The production office had only a telegraphic code address. The barman's cousin was not at all familiar with the Tahitian telegraphic code system. Indeed, he appeared to resent it with a vehemence I was unable to comprehend and finally he refused to discuss the matter at all.

We drove at some speed on the island's single dirt-track figure-eight highway. We twisted through fields of sugarcane and orange groves, passed waterfalls and rushing mountain streams. There appeared to be no highway code

—or if there was one, it was interpreted with originality by the happy-go-lucky Polynesians. Hundreds of bicycles careened drunkenly across the road, with small children clinging like limpets to crossbars, handlebars and pillions at adventurous angles.

Papeete was no more than a shanty town, probably every bit as primitive as when Paul Gauguin first saw it in the late 1800s. The whole place had a sense of careless defeat and peeling neglect. The lush vegetation seemed almost threatening; it overwhelmed houses, smothered verandas. Snakelike tendrils clutched at the very quayside. I was surprised to see a large steamship in the port; it seemed so incongruous amid such green primeval chaos.

Damian, by now not the only one feeling thoroughly bad-tempered, stayed in the car with the nervous nanny. I went in search of Metro-Goldwyn-Mayer.

Beyond a row of low frame-built stores, containing endless rows of tins, leaking sacks of dried goods, and a swarm of industrious Chinese, was a bar. At a group of small tables set out on the unsteady veranda was a group of Europeans. My heart leaped. (Although I quickly learned that the term "European," used by the British to separate the natives from the white man, was not going to get me very far in the South Pacific.) They were American newspapermen covering the film. Richard, they thought, might be staying at the Hotel Tahiti. Addresses did not exist on the island; you were simply told how many kilometers a place was from Papeete and approximately in which direction it lay. We set out with renewed hope. Richard was not at the Hotel Tahiti. They suggested another hotel seventeen kilometers on.

This hotel was a complex of small huts built around a larger hut in a coconut grove on the edge of the seashore. Yes, the smiling receptionist told me, Mr. Harris was a guest . . . but he was away at sea. He did not know when he would return. "Shooting at sea," he said with professional authority rare in the hotel trade. "Very unpredictable."

We were not expected. After a great deal of discussion, it was decided that I could share Richard's small single hut with Damian; and an even smaller hut was found for the nanny. The nanny, who had refrained from comment since her arrival in the Paradise of the Pacific, found her tongue. "It is very different," she said, "from Wales." It sounded somehow ominous. I suddenly remembered she need give me only a week's notice. Fortunately, I was much too tired to let it worry me. I went straight to bed.

It seemed like only minutes later (it was in fact almost eight hours) I awoke to see Richard looking down on us cuddled up in his narrow bed. We had a happy tearful reunion. The French postmistress had misread my four for a seven in the cable I had sent; Richard had planned a reception for us on December 27 complete with a house to move into.

Christmas Day, as nanny was the first to admit, was different. It rained so heavily that we were forced to stay cooped up in our tiny hut until lunchtime. It was a new hotel and some of the utilities—particularly the plumbing arrangements—were as yet imperfect. The drainage was of a primitive ditch design, uncovered and prone to overflowing in an alarming fashion. It stopped raining for a moment around lunchtime and we made our way to the big hut which served as bar, games room, reception area and dining room. There we had our Christmas dinner of hamburgers, chips and Coke. My folding Christmas tree completed the festive picture.

Richard was delighted when I told him about the baby. He wanted a large family. He told the news to anyone who would listen, adding that it had better arrive with a mass of red hair, a broken nose, and swearing like a trooper—"otherwise it isn't mine." Ignoring this admonitory remark, I hoped that his specifications were discardable if we happened to have a daughter.

All was not well on the picture. There were so many people blaming people. God help the executive in charge of the weather. Noah could have comfortably launched his ark even in one of the lighter showers.

Our house, fifteen kilometers from the capital, chief port and business center, was considered one of the finest on the island. By Tahitian standards it probably was very fine indeed. Certainly it was beautifully located on the beach, surrounded by high coconut trees which swayed gracefully in the wind.

The house was unfortunately plagued with cockroaches and rats. The rats were audibly at home in the rafters and had to be submitted to weekly doses of poison; the cockroaches were more apparent and one had to tread gingerly so as not to squash them under one's feet in the mornings.

The generator had been built next to the rubbish tip at the end of the garden. Since the generator had to be switched to off every night, the journey into that area was nightmarish. Scorpions, land crabs, rats, slugs, weasels and all sorts of loathsome things infested that spot. I am frankly squeamish. I can get quite hysterical at the sight of a spider in the bath. Having to make that nocturnal journey to the generator was my idea of hell. Richard was not much braver, but a good deal noisier. His method of dealing with the generator and the surrounding livestock was to shout, sing, curse and cry at the top of his voice there and back. He made it sound like a one-man commando raid.

At a New Year's Eve party in Papeete, I met Marlon Brando for the first time. He was an attractive, sensual-looking man with eyes that seemed to look right into you.

"Are you faithful to Richard?" he asked me almost at once.

"Yes," I said, surprised at his instant intimacy.

"You can't be," he said. "You answered too quickly."

"It is a question that doesn't require reflection," I said stiffly.

He didn't say anything to that. He sat and watched me for a long time, drinking in a careful steady way.

Later he told Richard in his ventriloquist's voice, "You're a lucky man. You've a faithful wife."

Brando was a man who never gave a clue to what he was really thinking, even when the drink was flowing and dangerous confidences are so easily swapped. There was a sense of isolation about him nearly all the time, not quite shyness and not quite arrogance either. He carried a book most of the time, which suddenly engrossed him whenever he wished to avoid conversation.

On the surface Richard and Marlon appeared to get on all right, although I didn't feel they were ever relaxed together. Richard kept his distance. Still, he admired Marlon as an actor enormously and looked forward to their scenes together.

I was now beginning to faint fairly regularly and had entered the craving stage of my pregnancy. I passionately wanted steamed treacle pudding and rock cakes. The local shopkeeper, a Chinese fellow proud of his exotic and extraordinary range of foodstuffs, was flummoxed. Unable to comprehend treacle pudding, let alone purvey it, he lost face. He did not take kindly to my visits; he became not so much inscrutable as invisible. My orders were

relayed through a somewhat backward child of eight. It
did not make marketing in Tahiti any easier.

I had always hated being examined during my previous
pregnancy; this time I looked forward to my prenatal ap-
pointments with joy. The surgery was the only air-condi-
tioned room on the island. The hospital itself terrified me.
Crowded, airless, smelling of the sick and rotting vegetation. I was determined not to end up there.

The production was going too slowly. The weather continued to be foul. Tension on the set was getting worse as
the picture fell further and further behind schedule and
went more and more over the budget. There had to be a
scapegoat. Rumors were rife that the studio was getting
ready to sack Carol Reed, the English director, who ulti-
mately resigned. The British actors, incensed and loyal,
were threatening not to work if such a move were made;
since no one was able to work anyway, I thought this
wasn't much of a threat.

It was now the beginning of a new year, 1961. The actors were homesick and lonely, 12,000 miles from England and virtually cut off from contact with the outside
world. The London newspapers arrived weeks late; there
were no telephones; and the local radio stations failed to
show any interest in outside events. To make things a little cozier I started to keep open house. Gordon Jackson,
Percy Herbert, Noel Purcell and Eddie Byrne came over
to enjoy what vaguely resembled home cooking. Cooking,
unfortunately, is not among my most notable accomplishments.

In such a close community it is easy to get things out of
perspective and sometimes relationships—both loving and
loathing—get exaggerated. Most people assumed that
Noel Purcell and Eddie Byrne were bosom pals. They
were both from Dublin, had appeared together many

times in the theater and in films. One would therefore
never ask one to dinner without extending an invitation
to the other. Thus, they went everywhere together.

"For Christ's sake, Elizabeth," Eddie Byrne came out
with it one evening. "Can't you ever ask me to dinner
without asking Noel? We can't stand the sight of each
other. Until we worked on this awful friggin' picture we
hadn't spoken to each other in Dublin for ten years."

During my time in Tahiti I made two genuine friends:
Phil and Marie Rhodes. Phil was Marlon's personal
makeup man; and his wife Marie, Marlon's stand-in. They
had all shared an apartment in New York in the early
days, long before Marlon became a success in *Streetcar
Named Desire*. They had helped the young Marlon and
now they worked on every movie he made.

I turned to Marie a lot during those months; she was
used to living in difficult locations and helped me cope.
One evening we were having a drink at a bar in the port
with Phil, Marie and Marlon when the quiet was interrupted by the arrival of a large and happy party from
Lancashire, improbably taking a package cruise through
the Society Islands. They recognized Richard and
crowded around our table asking for autographs and taking pictures. Nobody recognized Marlon. However,
clearly not wishing to hurt anyone's feelings, they thrust
their autograph books into everybody's hands and we
were all told to sign. Looking back, I don't think that
Marlon *wanted* to be recognized. He did not exert his
personality at all. It was as if he chose to be faceless.
Tahiti was his sanctuary, his refuge. He could wander
where he pleased in Papeete without being pestered,
without attracting attention. He spoke excellent French
and talked easily with most of the people there.

The only other person besides Marlon who didn't appear in any great hurry to return to Los Angeles, or to anywhere else for that matter, was Hugh Griffith. He was a large, dark, combustious Welshman, with big round protruding eyes. He had become rather more native than the natives. Informality was the going style; Mr. Griffith, always willing to extend the frontiers of fashion, turned up at one beach party in his tanned birthday suit.

6. *Everybody's Talking About Richard*

We returned to Los Angeles. I couldn't help wondering what the Tahitians who had accompanied us would make of that city. They were used to sharing, in a haphazard fashion, one uncomplicated, underdeveloped road. In Los Angeles they found themselves on a freeway with massive highways in all directions. Traffic signals must have seemed a mysterious adornment. The Chieftain and Tarita, Brando's girl friend, were among the Tahitians brought back. They spoke a little French but no English. I was told that Tarita's father had sold cows to pay her fare from Bora Bora to Tahiti when her boy friend, a cook at one of the hotels, heard they were auditioning for girls to dance the *tamori*. She was finally picked to play Marlon's woman.

The American diet was vastly different from what they had been used to in Tahiti. The studio became alarmed when Tarita's face blew up and bumps appeared. They discovered this was due to her partiality to chocolates. Boxes of them. Big boxes. The Chieftain was rushed to the hospital after collapsing. He had eaten, in one sitting, twenty hamburgers. He was only a little Chieftain.

We rented a pretty house on Bedford Drive in Beverly Hills that Jason Robards and Lauren Bacall had just vacated. At first I found it disconcerting that most of our guests knew the house better than we did. I got used to it in the end; it was simply part of the transitory style of Hollywood life. Certainly we were now living in true Hollywood style. This time our house was in the right area; we had the required acreage of pool, a large car (I had now passed my test), a cook, maid and nanny.

We were not the only ones to wonder how the hell we were paying for it.

Los Angeles had a sense of vitality. There was so much happening. We saw Bob and Dorothy Mitchum again. We made new friends, including Morti and Margi Guterman. Morti has the biggest agency for lighting cameramen in Hollywood and is consequently one of the best informed men in town. In Hollywood to be uninformed is to be dead. The Gutermans became two of my most constant friends and Margi a friend I grew to love.

Larry Harvey was now living in L.A. in sumptuous style. His marriage to Margaret Leighton was over; his friendship with Joan Cohn, the widow of Columbia film boss Harry Cohn, was the newest and most talked about romance in town. Larry's connections were amazing and he generously introduced us to everyone.

"Contacts, dear heart," he would say, "are everything. Talent is nothing without a studio head or two in your pool." He was a funny, cynical, generous man and I felt sad when he later fell out with Richard over *Camelot*. Larry had had a tremendous personal success in the London production and dearly wanted to do the movie; he never forgave Richard for getting that part. Fortunately I

remained his friend until his untimely death in 1973. I
shall never forget the kindnesses he showed us. One weekend he invited us to stay at a beautiful house he had just
finished building in Palm Springs. Richard and I wanted
to visit a nearby Indian reservation but because of the intense heat in the desert decided to wait until the evening.
"Don't be late for dinner," Joan told us as we set off. "We
have interesting guests coming—and a surprise for you."

I have often kicked myself for being unpunctual, but
never more than I did that evening in Palm Springs. As
we arrived back at the house, a large dark limousine, its
smoked windows closed tight, pulled away.

"We told you not to be late," Larry said. "There goes
the surprise. Garbo."

It is odd how great a pull Greta Garbo still has, even in
a town where nobody is elevated to pedestal height until
the obituary notices are out.

Larry's hospitality helped us bear our disappointment.
It was a night to remember. Joan was looking especially
glamorous that evening in a blue Givenchy gown; the
candlelight reflected brilliantly the diamonds she wore
around her neck and in her ears. We dined outside; all
around us was the peculiar silence of the desert. I was
completely taken by surprise when Richard and Larry
suddenly threw Joan into the pool—Givenchy and all.
They dived in after her—but not, I noticed, before Larry
had carefully removed his Cartier watch.

God Almighty, she'll kill the pair of them, I thought.
The following day was Sunday; there would be no way
she could get her hair fixed. And Joan Cohn is a very im-
maculate woman. I waited for the explosion.

She came to the surface slowly. She was smiling.

"You two had better start diving," she said coolly, her
beautiful coiffured hair hanging in straggly strands about

her shoulders. "I've lost my earrings. They are of no senti-
mental value, just very valuable."

That, I thought, was real style.

It was a lovely weekend and gave Richard a chance to
get away from the rows and the tensions at MGM. The
picture continued to go badly. Carol Reed, as predicted,
had been replaced by the veteran director Lewis Mile-
stone. The script, Richard complained, changed hourly.
He was drinking heavily again. We seemed to start
fighting over nothing.

One afternoon Marlon called and asked me to bring
Damian to his house for tea and to meet his son, Chris-
tian. They were both the same age, almost three. Marlon
was fond of children. He had always taken time to say a
few words to Damian whenever I had taken him on the
set. Once he asked Damian where he lived. With a deep
sigh he answered, "In an alowplane."

Marlon played with the children for hours that afternoon. He had a Japanese-style home and all visitors had
to remove their shoes before entering. The floors were
highly polished. The boys wanted to ride their tricycles
inside. I protested but Marlon said it was fine. He pa-
tiently followed them around with a cloth, wiping away
the offending tire marks. It was a strange and curiously
moving contrast to the unapproachable star at the studios.

Richard and Marlon, always wary of each other, were
now openly hostile. A feud with Marlon might have made
life uncomfortable on the set but it also made very good
copy for the newspaper. Richard played it up outra-
geously.

In one scene Marlon had to knock Richard to the
ground. Richard complained that Marlon's punch was too
light and refused to go down. Marlon's second punch,

Richard claimed, made no greater impact. He kissed Marlon lightly on the cheek, saying, "Shall we dance?"

Richard was not simply showing off. He genuinely believed that he had to stand up to Marlon if he wasn't going to be completely outmaneuvered in their scenes together. Richard had spent a lot of time on the set watching Marlon work. He acknowledged he could learn a lot from Marlon, but more than that he wanted to know how to handle himself when they came to their scenes together. Hollywood acting at that level is not unlike prizefighting. It is important to know the other actor's moves, to be prepared for his feints and wiles and bag of tricks. Richard was impressed with Marlon's brand of professionalism. During rehearsals Marlon would go over the top, encouraging the other players to respond with matching loud performances. In the take, Marlon would suddenly underplay the scene . . . paring down his gestures, lowering his voice, softening his tone. "He slips under your guard," said Richard, satisfied. "I can deal with that."

Richard was full of wicked stories about Marlon's Method. He was particularly pleased when Marlon (according to Richard) insisted on being smothered in ice beneath the blanket to make him shiver realistically in his death scene. "Imagine that now," said Richard in mock wonderment. "Imagine that."

My mother came to visit us. Her trip was cut short, however, since the whole *Mutiny* production was moved back to Tahiti for some new scenes. My baby was now well on the way. It wasn't safe for me to return and I decided to go straight to London with Damian. On our last night in our home on Bedford Drive, my mother met Hugh Griffith and Robert Mitchum. Both in their different ways left a lasting impression upon her.

Hugh arrived in a suspiciously merry mood. He was particularly pleased with a painting he had just completed and we were invited to his house for a preview. The canvas, he said, was too large to carry with him. He was not exaggerating. Painted onto an extremely large Early American wardrobe was the reclining naked figure of a voluptuous woman, amply displaying her charms. The truly three-dimensional realism of the work was due not so much to Hugh's accomplishments as an artist as to his artful arrangement of two doorknobs about the lady's anatomy. The fact that the wardrobe was a rather expensive antique belonging to somebody else did not appear to worry Hugh at all. Indeed, he was genuinely grieved that he would have to leave his masterpiece behind when his lease was up.

Bob Mitchum came to wish us bon voyage and stayed late into the night. On her way to bed, my mother remarked that she would get a hot-water bottle, as her neck felt stiff. Bob, whose accomplishments are varied and surprising, offered to give her a massage.

She nervously declined.

"Siddown, lady. Put your ass over here," he said.

She obeyed without a murmur. Bob gave her a professional pounding.

"No lady," he said, "should go to bed with a hot-water bottle. It isn't couth."

It was four months before Richard and I were to meet again. During that time I gave birth to our second son, Jared, who arrived (as ordered) with a mass of red hair. For several months, Richard had to make do with photographs of his new son, who was too delicate to travel to the States. Damian and I did return for a while, leaving Jared in the care of my parents.

Richard had rented, on a weekly basis, Boris Karloff's

old home. It was a gloomy, rambling Spanish-style house built on two stories with a balcony running around the top floor which overlooked a courtyard. In the courtyard was a large rectangular pool.

We had many boisterous parties and friends in that house. One of the most boisterous visitors of all was an Irishman by the name of Malachy McCourt. He had a habit of dropping in unexpectedly from New York, where he owned a notable bar. He was a big distinctive-looking man with a large bushy red beard and long red hair. He loved to swim in the pool.

Looking up into the hills one morning, I saw a pall of black smoke rising hundreds of feet into the sky. Fire, always a threat in California in the dry summer months, was spreading rapidly. Wild animals were soon plunging into pools to avoid the flames. People threw their silver and jewelry into their pools before fleeing from the holocaust. There was a great deal of chaos. Hundreds of people lost their homes in that fire, including the people from whom we rented the old Karloff house. Naturally they wanted their house back as soon as possible and we moved into the Bel Air Hotel. We had no time to tell anyone of our change of address.

The American family, relieved to be back in their own home after the ordeal of the fire, were not prepared for the sight that greeted them the following morning. On going to the balcony they gazed down on the pool. There floating on an air mattress was the peaceful sleeping figure of Malachy McCourt.

When *Mutiny on the Bounty* was finally released, Richard's named appeared above the title along with Trevor Howard and Marlon Brando. Robert Mitchum said it was incredible. Wherever he went in Hollywood, people were talking about Richard. In all the studios, at parties, in the restaurants and the clubs, the talk was of Richard Harris. "Everybody is asking," said Bob, "who the fuck is Richard Harris?"

During those interminable months in Tahiti, the director Lindsay Anderson had been backward and forward to discuss a picture he wanted to make with Richard. It was David Storey's *This Sporting Life*. Lindsay wanted Richard to play Frank Machin, a fuming, inarticulate Yorkshire rugby league player. It was a meaty role and Richard was naturally enthusiastic. They spent weeks working out their ideas, Richard and Lindsay. By the time Richard returned to London, the picture was ready to go. Rachel Roberts had been signed to play Mrs. Hammond, Machin's landlady and mistress.

Richard got on well with Rachel, although they were dangerously alike in many ways. Spirited, volatile and outspoken, they were never in any doubt about what each other wanted and thought. Rachel had just married Rex Harrison. At the end of shooting there was a party on the set and both Rex and I were invited. I felt again an uneasiness in his presence and completely tongue-tied, although he was perfectly agreeable in a rather abstracted fashion. He and Richard didn't have very much to say to each other. As I looked at them I thought how they were totally different types of actors, different kinds of men. They had nothing in common.

Lindsay Anderson was a patient and painstaking director. He became one of Richard's closest friends and was always willing to advise and help. He was loyal, possessive, erudite. His taste and knowledge encouraged a new dimension within Richard. They would fight and argue; Richard was always impressed with Lindsay's intellectual brawn. I liked Lindsay, even if sometimes I did resent his tendency to monopolize Richard. But I knew he was good for Richard and encouraged their friendship. It was not always easy. I know that Lindsay (like J. P. Donleavy perhaps) thought that I was too frivolous. He was inclined to reply to any opinion I might venture with a small shrug and a curt "Well of course, that is exactly what I would expect *you* to say." He seemed to have serious reservations about my intellectual capacity.

Lindsay was and is an Establishment rebel. I suspected he considered me to belong to, and behave like, an Establishment woman. I had long ago given up the luxury of such a debate. I was just trying to survive. However, he did try to keep the peace between Richard and me in our ever-increasing rows and I was thankful for that. I think he genuinely felt I was an important stabilizing influence in Richard's life and that the children and I provided him with a home background that he needed.

But I was actually beginning to get a bit brassed off with my role. Providing the background color was beginning to make me feel very old—although I realized that there were people who didn't consider reaching their twenty-fifth birthday as being over the hill.

During the making of *This Sporting Life*, I discovered I was again pregnant. My maternity clothes had barely been returned from the cleaners. The Catholic side of the family took the news in their stride; the Welsh, nonconformists, on the other hand, were not used to reproducing themselves at such a rate and were alarmed in case our enthusiasm got out of hand.

Our growing family had done nothing to settle Richard's old restless nettlesome ways. We were, or so the petition to have us removed from our flat in Allen House stated, a wild, noisy, drunken household. We were rapidly lowering the tone of the Establishment, if not of the whole neighborhood. They did have a point. In order to

successfully remove us from our flat, the determined petitioners had to secure the signatures of the tenants on either side of us. Although everyone in the block had en-
thusiastically signed the document (some of them several
times, judging by its inordinate length), the neighbor on
our left firmly declined to contribute his vital signature.
His name was Peter Jeffreys and he owned a large print-
ing works in Penge. He was also, and more to the point,
one of Richard's drinking companions in the local pub,
the Britannia. Many a morning our loyal and cheerful
neighbor would arrive carrying a bottle of champagne for
breakfast . . . this could be any hour before 2 P.M. He
felt that everyone needed in the morning what he called a
"heart starter."

The failed petitioners, however, were about to get a
lucky break. With another baby on the way, we had to
look for larger premises. Only we faced a tricky problem.
References. We would need them for an unfurnished
apartment, and certainly our present landlords were unlikely to give us much of a recommendation.

While we pondered this apparently insoluble problem,
we took a three-month lease on a furnished house in a
hitherto quiet road in Kensington.

This time I was to have my baby in style in a private
nursing home. The night before I was due to go in to
have the baby induced, Richard serenaded me and the
rest of the street the entire night. I sensed that the peti-
tions would be flying again the next morning. "The parties they be small, they be small," he sang. "And we eat
them skin and all, skin and all." I left him sitting on the
pavement, giving his all. I was getting up and preparing
my departure to the nursing home when he passed me in
the hall, his eyes shining like very small red marbles.

When he finally located me, and the nursing home, I was in labor. I told him that I needed a doctor. The pains were getting frequent, but the nurse insisted I was being ridiculous. She told me I would be hours yet and left the room. I was in the usual sort of pain, making the usual sort of noises most women make in these conditions. Suddenly from beneath the sheets came a loud demanding cry.

We both went pale.

Richard went roaring out of the room shouting for a doctor. I could hear him cursing the nursing home, the nurses and the whole damned medical profession as he disappeared down the corridor.

When the rumpus had died down I discovered I had given birth to an eight-and-a-half-pound baby boy. His sunny nature was not at all impaired by his rowdy entrance into the world. We called him Jamie.

7. Starve the Man

A nearby house in Bedford Gardens was up for sale at a reasonable price. I suggested that we should try to buy it. After some persuasion the bank manager advanced us a loan guaranteed by my father. It was a large family house with two commendable features. A large cherry tree in the back garden and a large cherry tree in the front garden. By no amount of imagination could the house be described as beautiful. It was the kind of house that estate agents in desperation describe as "a building of unusual character." It was tall, ugly, with two poky rooms arranged on each of five floors. No sooner had I settled in than I was off again to join Richard in Italy, where he had landed a role in an Antonioni film, *The Red Desert*.

Richard's excitement at working with Michelangelo Antonioni had turned to disenchantment. Antonioni made no secret of the fact that he preferred to work with amateurs. He developed quaint passions for people he met on the streets whose faces would fit in with a particular landscape or decor. Richard found him baffling. He called him "a genius, but mad." The total lack of understanding between them was predictable. Antonioni didn't speak any English. Richard had no knowledge of Italian or French. Their conversations were limited to mime and gestures open to a large variety of interpretation.

Antonioni looked and was autocratic. His skin was the color of parchment; his whole personality reminded me of old parchment. It was as if all life had dried up within him. He fascinated me. He gave no indication of his brilliance and exciting imagination.

Things were happening quickly now. Richard flew to California to begin another picture.

In the night I had a telephone call from Jerry Bresler, his new producer. "Richard has collapsed, Elizabeth. He is suffering from severe exhaustion. He is in the hospital under sedation and sleeping like a baby. He'll be fine in a few days."

Minutes later, Richard was on the line. Cursing, shouting, complaining and altogether bloody furious that I hadn't been in touch!

"I've only just this minute heard, Richard!" I pointed out indignantly.

"It isn't good enough," he roared. "It isn't fucking good enough at all."

Sleeping like a baby! Under sedation! I should have known better than to believe that.

I agreed to join him in Mexico when the production moved to Cuernavaca. I loved Mexico. I adored the extravagant colors, the sense of history, the simple raw beauty of the land. The intense poverty at first blinded me to this, but after a while the constant assault on one's conscience was dulled by the familiarity of so much want.

Richard did not hit it off with Charlton Heston. Chuck —or Chuckles, as he was known in our household—was

not amused by Richard. Richard was not impressed by
Heston's solemnity. "He is so square," he complained. "He
came out of a cubic womb."

Richard got on much better with James Coburn. One
afternoon the three of us went to the bullfights at the
Plaza de Toros in Mexico City. The first fight had ended
badly. The matador had lost his nerve and fled from the
arena without a backward glance. The crowd was furious.
Cushions, fruit, hats, bottles and even shoes were hurled
into the ring. A Mexican sitting in front of us didn't find
the incident half as amusing as we evidently did. He
turned in his seat and deliberately knocked Richard's bag
of sweets off the rail.

"Did you see that? Look at that, will you?" Richard was
on his feet, appealing to the crowd with gladiatorial
gusto. "Godammit, look at what that fellow has done to
me sweets!"

Nothing much was happening in the untidy bullring.
The spirited Mexican crowd encouraged Richard in his
magnificent rage. The affair ended abruptly when Richard, bored with his own rhetoric, delivered a blow to
the aficionado's chin. It was Richard's view that summary
violence against certain people was legitimate and far
more effective than rational discussion.

Lindsay Anderson visited us in Cuernavaca. We decided each to make an 8mm film of our impressions of
Mexico. Lindsay's film showed the color of the country. I
concentrated on the people. Richard filmed a child's funeral.

Death has always preoccupied Richard, just as it preoc-
cupies my father. It has never worried me. Just as getting
old has never really worried me. I don't relish old age, but
I don't let it get me down either. If I lived to be a hun-

dred I couldn't feel older than I felt at twenty-five. I felt jammed in. I knew that I belonged to a generation that was out of step. I had been brought up to believe that if we played the Establishment game, obeyed the Establishment rules, one day we would be given the Establishment prizes. Only by prize-giving day the Establishment would no longer be around. I could see the end of the season; I just didn't know what to sow for the season to follow.

I wanted my sons to know the Establishment world, to be educated in Establishment schools and to see a life outside the film studios. Later I hoped that if they enjoyed the benefits of both worlds they could choose for themselves where they felt most at home.

The power to forget is sometimes as important as the power to remember. I now find it difficult to relate to the woman I was then. I look at photographs taken of me at that time and the woman in them is a stranger to me. I only remember being squeezed and suffocated and somehow reduced.

The house was bursting with Richard. People came to talk to Richard. People telephoned Richard. People discussed Richard and listened to Richard. The house was organized for Richard. Richard was fond of telling people that I was marvelous: "Her sole job is to keep me alive, and she does that very well."

I didn't want that to be my sole job. I was beginning to resent his attitude, his presumptuous sense of proprietorship. I wanted to be *me*. Only I was weak. I never stood up to him.

We spent most of that summer in Rome. Richard was making a picture with Princess Soraya. Richard's tendency to call her Soya, as in sauce, upset studio courtiers a lot. It was suggested that he call her Your Highness. He agreed on condition that she address my brother Morgan, who was accompanying him, as the Honorable Morgan. The bargain was struck. "Would the Honorable Morgan like a drink?" the Princess would inquire punctiliously.

I was looking forward to meeting her myself. Curiously Richard refused to accept any of her invitations during my time in Rome; nor did he press any invitations upon her. It was the only film he ever made during which I wasn't asked to the set or to any of the parties. I thought this was peculiarly unfriendly. The film turned out to be a disaster; it wasn't shown outside Italy. Princess Soraya retired from the performing arts after that. I was sorry that I never got a chance to see them in action together.

Still, there were moments when the marriage worked. But they were rare. I was becoming afraid of Richard. I was scared of his sudden anger and his violence. It was short-lived, his wrath, but it was rough while it lasted.

A lot of Richard's friends were now people I didn't know and never met. He had a life apart. I felt that there were other women. When he stayed out all night, I accepted whatever explanation he chose to give me. I gave him a lot of rope. I didn't have the courage to do otherwise. I clung to my naïveté. Naïveté can also be a kind of comfort.

We were seldom alone together now. I welcomed the anonymity that the crowd in my home gave me. The house was always full of people, mostly strangers; it seemed years since I had had a conversation with anyone. The life I had known when I first met Richard belonged to another age; I had lost touch with all my old friends. I was in a strange, disturbing void. I didn't feel at home anywhere.

Richard told me once that a person had always to do what he wanted to do and to hell with anyone else. I had argued that this could never work—unless one lived alone and selfishly. Now I was beginning to see the merits of his argument. I knew then that it was I who was changing, and not Richard. He had never promised me any life other than the one we were leading. He had been consistent in that.

So many of the people around Richard now were sycophants and cadgers. Actors are surrounded by people who make a living out of them in one way or another: it isn't surprising that actors sometimes lose sight of themselves. Pretty soon they start believing their own publicity and being taken in by their own inventions.

I wouldn't have said that to Richard then, even if I'd had the courage. It would have sounded like sour grapes. And I could never be sure that there wouldn't have been an element of truth in such an accusation.

On the surface our lives went on in much the same way. But Richard and his work were moving deeper into the background of my thoughts: he had lost his priority in my life. On the surface I went along with whatever was happening. I fell in dutifully with all his plans; I made all the right noises; I jumped through the old accustomed hoops.

Only I knew the conviction had gone.

If Richard suspected any of this he never discussed it. We now had no financial worries. Richard was making movie after movie, Hollywood productions that paid very handsomely. He bought a dark blue Rolls-Royce, complete with fitted bar. He had to find new chauffeurs almost as often as he had to replenish the bar. Chauffeurs, especially Rolls chauffeurs, were confounded by his casual ways and woozy charm. He had a disturbing habit of kissing his driver good night and greeting him the morning after with a stream of obscenities and an irrational kick up the arse.

All the cars that we had owned before had been *ours*. The Rolls was different. The Rolls was definitely *his*. I've noticed men tend to get very possessive about their Rolls-Royces.

I had a very generous dress allowance. He allowed me to attend the Paris collections; I became familiar with the salons of Yves St. Laurent, Nina Ricci, Balenciaga. Flying to Paris for fittings was a far cry from the blue serge curtains of my mother's maid's room.

He continued to help his family in Ireland. He gave the money he had earned from Rank Films on *This Sporting Life* to Rank Flour Mills in Limerick to keep them from closing down his father's mills. His father was very ill and had no idea how bad the situation was. He never did find out. The day after his funeral, the receivers moved in.

Richard's next big movie was *Hawaii*. He was now beginning to collect a regular entourage around him. We took a splendid house in Diamond Head Road, the most fashionable area of Honolulu.

We now had an excess of comforts, including a large swimming pool, tennis courts and plenty of servants to see to our needs. We had survived the hard times, and now we had the job of surviving success.

I spent most of the day with the children and most of the evenings on my own. Richard told me he had to do a lot of night shooting. Later I learned that most of his night work was conducted at a nearby hotel and those scenes had nothing to do with the movie. Now he was again taking flight in alcohol.

The drinks they served in Honolulu were very strong! One of his favorite beverages was called Mai Tai. I don't

know if this concoction was stronger than the drink he
had been used to, but it had a very unpleasant effect on
him. Richard's drinking and Richard's fights were becoming well-known on the island and we were not welcomed
everywhere. It was embarrassing, limiting and very boor-
ish.

Richard was becoming intensely self-absorbed. He
seemed to be preoccupied by his own responses to himself. Sometimes this led him to the brink of self-parody.
Only it wasn't very amusing any more. I felt more than
ever that we were being irrevocably forced apart by emotional chaos and a paranoia I didn't understand. My own
grip on any emotion except fear was tentative. An imagined slight, a joke that misfired, a misunderstood remark
. . . all were enough to spark off a terrifying violent rage
within him.

I knew all the danger signals. His very appearance
would change in an alarming fashion. A hard-boiled look
came into his eyes; his face grew taut. His voice took on a
sharp cutting edge as he started to speak in a deliberate
manner. When that happened I knew that all hell was
about to break loose. Anything in his path would be
smashed—including human beings.

One of his favorite sports was to go into the road and
attack passing cars with his bare fists.

In Spain some time before, after a quiet dinner in the
hills, we were returning by taxi to Valencia when out of
the blue he went berserk. He started smashing the windows of the taxi and kicking in the dashboard and mir-
ror. I was terrified. I screamed at the driver to stop the
car. Richard leaped out and ran into the night, his hands
pouring with blood. He stopped in the middle of the
highway. Lorries and cars hurtled by, their horns blar-
ing and lights flashing. Astonished drivers screamed abu-

sive advice at him. He stood his ground, defying them to run him down. A few drivers slowed down to witness the spectacle, others stopped completely. The lorries that stopped he beat with his fists. It was an amazing scene. Drivers sat there in wonderment until he tired. Then they drove off, shaking their heads.

There was nothing I could do. I watched him run back to a little village we had just passed. When I caught up with him he was pounding and kicking a large oak door, the entrance to a courtyard. I could not imagine why he had it in for that door. After a while, the door opened a few inches and a little old lady in black peered out, then closed the door again. Within seconds she reopened the door and stepped outside onto the pavement. She had brought with her a chair which she now placed alarmingly close to Richard. Without a murmur, her face expressionless, she watched while he went on attacking the door. She seemed sympathetic toward him. She seemed to understand what hell he was suffering, what demons were driving him.

After a while he got back into the car and we returned to our hotel. That evening was never mentioned again.

I feared for Richard on that island. One night I awoke to discover that Richard was taking on the traffic on Diamond Head Road. I went back into the house and telephoned the hospital. I explained as carefully as I could that my husband was very upset. I asked them to send a doctor to give him something to quiet him down. It seems that in Hawaii if you ask a hospital to send a doctor or an ambulance, the police are automatically informed. I explained that this was a private matter and that we didn't need the police. They absolutely refused to send one without the other. While I was trying to change their minds, Richard came into the room. I quickly put down the telephone. I was very scared.

"What the fuck are you up to?"

It was useless to lie to him. He came toward me. A bolt of fear paralyzed me. I waited for the rage to engulf me. It never came.

Frank Harper, Richard's stand-in and drinking companion, mercifully got in between us.

To see such big men fight so furiously is frightening. It was very brave of Harper to defend me against Richard. He was in a tricky position: he knew he could not damage Richard, who had to film the next day; he had to subdue him without disturbing his profile. Richard had no such reluctance and hit out forcefully. I suddenly understood the Russian proverb: In a fight the rich man tries to save his face, the poor man his coat.

What should have been the most marvelous time of our lives had become a nightmare. We had three healthy children. Richard had success and fame. We had money. I had read somewhere that an actor has to starve the man to feed the star. It was a frightening thought. My fear of Richard was turning into hate. My only thoughts now were of keeping out of his way. The animal quality that I had found so exciting when I first met him now sickened me.

I longed only to be with a man who was quiet, gentle, and whose every thought and word were completely predictable. The time for me to return to London couldn't come quickly enough and I thanked God when Richard had to return to Los Angeles for extra studio scenes. I returned home feeling as if I had been given a reprieve.

The reprieve was for a limited time only. I didn't have the courage to make the final break. I was now twenty-eight. Richard had become a way of life, as well as my husband. My only contact with the outside world was through him. I had completely lost my confidence as well as my old *joie de vivre*. I knew I had to leave him; I just didn't know how to.

In London we were living a fairly social life. One evening at a dinner party at the writer Ivan Moffett's (Princess Margaret was there and Richard, impressed with the Royal family, was perfectly correct and dutifully amusing), I met Robin Douglas-Home. Nephew of an archetypal Tory Prime Minister, he was nightclub pianist and newspaper columnist; he was everything that Richard was not. Robin was the supreme advocate of Annabels and Ascot. He asked me to tea at the Ritz. He was amusing, attentive and, what was more important, he found me attractive—and wasn't afraid to say so.

I had been with Richard nine years. During that time I had never once been unfaithful to him. Now I developed an intemperate passion for an entirely unsuitable man. The fact that I could feel anything for anyone other than Richard shocked me. My experience with Robin was not that important or that happy. But it made me realize that I could be interested in someone other than my husband.

I behaved in a most neurotic manner. I had no experience in leading a double life. I wasn't very convincing in my new role. I knew that Richard was becoming increasingly suspicious. He would now want to know where I was going if I left the house for even a few hours, and who I spoke to on the phone. It was a time of maximum pressure.

A gambling man, Robin had got very deeply into debt. At least one smart London club, with too many of his markers, had seen fit to send their heavies after him. Robin came to me one evening at Bedford Gardens and said he needed £2,000 quickly. He was in a distraught

state and had been drinking heavily. I didn't have that
sort of money to lend him. There is nothing more distressing than a frightened man; I understood his fear. I knew
what he was going through. The following morning I
pawned a diamond bracelet and most of my rings for
£2,000 and gave it to him. I knew that it would be only
a temporary answer to his problems; it did not remove his
need to gamble again. I knew it was unlikely that he
would ever raise the money to pay me back; I never did
find the cash to redeem my pieces. Giving him the money
changed our relationship. After that loan we began to
drift apart and it was never quite the same again. The
money was never mentioned again. Early one evening in
October 1968, Robin telephoned me from Meadowbrook,
his cottage in Sussex. He asked me to go down for the
weekend; it was not possible, I told him. He pleaded with
me to change my mind, but it was impossible for me to
alter my arrangements. He had not been so anxious for
my company for a very long time indeed and I was
puzzled. I had no idea he was so desperate. That evening
he killed himself.

Richard and I lived apart for a while—pretending to
the press and in a sense to ourselves it wasn't happening.
It was easy to do. Richard was away a lot of the time on
various locations; when he returned he stayed in hotels.
He was usually on his best behavior when we met; he
kept his drinking under control.

It was during this period that we met the astrologer
Patric Walker at a dinner party Joan Thring was giving
for Rudolf Nureyev. Maybe if Patric had made some personal astrological calculations for that evening he would
have discovered a pressing engagement someplace else. A
man of volatile temperament, a ricochet wit and a sensible talent for contacts, Patric was brusquely indifferent

to anyone he didn't like. Richard took to him at once. He
has always had a high regard for people with style and
curiosity which leads them far and wide and astray. I
also liked Patric; but I recognized that you had to be
careful not to scratch his glossy surface.

Richard's interest in Patric was motivated somewhat
by self-interest. At that time he wanted more than anything to land the role of King Arthur in the movie of
Camelot. Richard Burton had played the role on Broadway, and Laurence Harvey had had a great personal success in the London production at Drury Lane. Richard
told Jack Warner, who was personally producing the film,
that he was prepared to test for the role: it was unheard
of for an actor of his experience to submit to a screen test.
What's more, Richard offered to pay for the test himself.
Warner, a man with a lot of respect for people willing to
save him money, agreed.

That evening at Joan Thring's Richard made an appointment for a private consultation with Patric. Patric
smartly predicted that Richard would get *Camelot*.
Richard was in a state of high tension; it made him querulous. "How do you know that?" he demanded. "You know
more than Jack Warner knows?"

"I'm telling you," Patric snapped, "Mr. Warner will go
with you."

"The odds are against it," Richard said gloomily.

"I'm an astrologer, not a wretched bookmaker," Patric
said. "If you want odds go to Ladbrokes. I only deal in
predictions."

Richard was too nervous to be encouraged. He suspected that Patric made predictions clients wanted to
hear the way some men make promises because people
seem to like promises. Keeping them was another matter.

"We'll see," Richard said. "We'll see."

Our marriage continued to be unsteady. Richard had his suspicions that I might have been unfaithful, but he still didn't know. I thought he did know. When he eventually asked me outright, I told him the truth. He reacted far more strongly than I ever imagined he would. I got to a telephone and called Patric Walker.

"Please come at once, Patric," I pleaded. He came, although the hour was late and he was confused about the role he was expected to play. Nevertheless, he was a calming influence. He persuaded Richard to go to bed.

"What started *that?*" he asked when Richard had retired. I told him what had happened. The advice Patric gave me had little to do with astrology but a great deal to do with common sense. "Never admit anything," he said. I swore I never would again; and I never did.

A few days after this episode, Richard heard that he had got *Camelot*. He was overwhelmed with happiness and relief. He felt it was a new beginning; he insisted that Patric and I accompany him to Hollywood. Patric would travel as his personal astrologer. It was a bizarre touch that emphasized Richard's determination to return to Hollywood in blazing style. We were to sail to New York on the *Queen Mary*, spend a week on the town, then fly to Los Angeles.

It was a plan that appealed to Patric's adagio sense of elegance immensely. His stateroom, filled with flowers and beautiful silver-framed photographs of those he loved, had an exquisite air of Edwardian propriety. His steward, Patric noted with satisfaction, laid out his velvet dinner jacket and silken finery with more than the customary Cunardian care. Clearly Patric had been recognized as a gentleman of distinction, a gentleman of breeding. "It is," he said to me, "going to be a memorable voyage."

The first night out we attended the Purser's cocktail party. In an exhilarated frame of mind we proceeded to dinner in the Verandah Grill. The meal had barely reached the second course when Richard showed disturbing signs of entering one of his bellicose moods. This side of Richard was new to Patric; sensibly and politely he said he was rather fatigued after all the excitement of our embarkation and hastened to his cabin.

Richard insisted on going to the bar for a nightcap. He also, alas, insisted on my company. Plans I had to jolly him out of his darkening mood were quickly ended. He was only just getting into his stride. His language was vivid and explicit. Within minutes he had inflated my single adventure in adultery into a cheap and dirty series of affairs. He could not see that my infidelity was almost accidental: I had succumbed not to excitement but to desperation. I was surprised by the incredible ease of it all, but now wasn't the time to debate the point. That familiar marbled look was coming into his eyes; he was beginning to speak in that deliberate manner.

I said I had to go to the ladies' room. I headed straight for Patric's cabin. He was in bed, reading *Nicholas and Alexandra*.

"I am beginning to see that you are a nocturnal lady," he observed, marvelously unruffled by my sudden appearance.

"Let me stay and talk to you for a while," I said. "Richard is getting worked up over that business with Robin Douglas-Home. I'll wait here until he cools down." I realized at once that Patric did not fully appreciate the hazards of living with Richard. "Don't be such a fool," he said in a gentle doctor-patient voice. "Of course Richard is bound to be a bit upset. No man takes kindly to his wife's indiscretion. But don't exaggerate the problem. Time cures everything . . ."

The door opened with such violence that it was a wonder it remained on its hinges. Patric was lifted out of his bed bodily and hurled across the cabin. He landed in a surprised silken heap; not daring to move a muscle, he watched Richard silently, systematically wreck the cabin. Flowers, silver picture frames, silk shirts, patent-leather pumps, hosiery, bedside trinkets, mementos filled the air in orbital fury.

Then, just as suddenly as he arrived, his anger spent, Richard left. Patric got to his feet and surveyed the debris. We looked at each other, neither of us caring to say a word. There was nothing we could say. Even "Good night" under the circumstances seemed out of place.

On each of the following five nights of that crossing the same thing happened. The days were always halcyon; Richard and Patric, apparently not men to harbor grudges, could be seen vigorously pacing the decks together, their conversation animated and eager. Richard entered into the spirit of all the ship's activities with gusto, charmingly courteous to fellow passengers and us alike.

Each day Patric convinced himself that Richard's excessive behavior the night before was the result of some temporary aberration that would not return. Each night Richard relapsed into his untactful ways.

Patric felt that my hiding place had been blown after the third night; he implored me to search for somewhere new to conceal myself. My imagination wasn't up to it, and the thought of Richard's ransacking the entire *Queen Mary* searching for my new sanctuary was unbearable. I continued to flee to Patric's bedraggled quarters.

Patric's steward was becoming noticeably nervous

about his Jekyll and Hyde passenger. Each morning without fail he would arrive with Patric's coffee to find his gentleman lying in a battered state, the room in shambles. Patric's reluctance to make any reference to the reduced circumstances in which he was now found each morning only added to the mystery.

Our stateroom, needless to say, remained a model of law and order.

I was so relieved to be off that boat.

Richard had agreed to do a movie with Doris Day before starting *Camelot*. He wasn't too ecstatic about it but *Camelot* was still some months off and we needed the money. We rented a magnificent house, the Villa Vesco in Bel Air. It was an extravagant setting for what were to be the most bizarre scenes of our marriage. Reality in that place never once intruded into our lives, or even into our thoughts.

8. Ghosts

Richard is not a man who suffers alone or in silence. When he had to be up at six in the morning to go to the studio, we *all* had to be up at six in the morning. Neither Patric nor I are morning creatures and our breakfast company lacked a sense of merriment. Still Richard insisted on our presence. It wasn't that our relationship had become close again; it was unnaturally intense. The emotional upheaval we had been through had to be lived and relived, as Richard endeavored to understand it.

He also expected us to be on call throughout the day; the only free time we had was between 7:30 A.M., when he left for makeup, and 9:30 A.M., when we had to report to the studio. The moment Richard was out of the front door, Patric would make for the bar and the vodka, I would head for the fridge and the orange juice. We would mix ourselves very strong, very large screwdrivers, turn up the music and dance around the hall and the pool, wafting across the lawns with gay abandon and through every room in the house. Patric said, "There's nothing left to do except laugh. It's like, there's Jewish humor, Irish humor or homosexual humor. You've got to be oppressed to be able to laugh." By the time we left for the studio we were human and happy again.

Patric's reputation had preceded him. His depraved adventures aboard the *Queen Mary* were known in Hollywood. Nobody believed that he was an astrologer; that was clearly a clever cover story. It was obvious to everyone that he was Richard's bodyguard and maybe his Svengali. Our first day on the set he was given the once-over by some very heavy-looking gentlemen apparently engaged to protect Miss Day from any untoward attention. Patric didn't find this as amusing as I did. He worried about his beautifully manicured fingernails; how much longer would they remain so unblemished and so long? After a few days his nerves were decidedly on edge; he even stopped wearing his dazzling diamond ring ("Mine was not an entirely misspent youth") for fear of some pre-emptive attack on his person.

I had in many ways a cosseted existence, although it was wearing having to account for every moment of the day to Richard. Men would arrive at the house to do my hair, fix my makeup, massage my body and anoint me with oils. Most evenings we attended some big party or other. Marvin Heims, a Beverly Hills jeweler, sent necklaces, earrings, bracelets and rings to complement the dresses I wore: emeralds for green, sapphires for blue, rubies for red and, of course, diamonds with everything. Most of these goodies were "on appro" and had to be returned the following morning. In Hollywood nearly everything is a hype.

As I swept down the long wide staircase one evening, I thought how timing is one of the most important things in life—and how sad it was that we have no control over that at all. Dressed in one of the most beautiful dresses money could buy, wearing exquisite jewelry, groomed by professionals, I was looking better than I had ever looked in my life. But now there was no one I was dressing up for. The thrill had gone.

I remembered the early days with Richard, the hungry days above the underwear shop in Earls Court, when I would make my own dresses out of sale remnants. I remembered the excitement I felt experimenting with something new I hoped would please him. Sometimes I would wear a flower or twist some material in my hair. I felt vital and alive then. He noticed me then.

Now as I came down that magnificent Hollywood staircase, I looked at him waiting for me. He looked more handsome now than in those days. But nothing mattered that much any more. How mean timing could be sometimes.

I was pampered and treated like a doll. Every evening, while I was bathing in the huge blue-and-gilt bathroom, my body reflected in a maze of tinted mirrors, Lubi the Mexican maid would serve me with iced champagne and hot canapés. She would help me dry with soft warm towels and help me into my negligee—a negligee costing what once took us a month to earn.

I never had to worry about food, or about household problems. Lubi and the butler Eduardo saw to everything. Eduardo inspected the waiters' hands, their nails, even their white gloves, before the start of any dinner party. The glass sparkled and the silver gleamed.

I wanted for nothing—except money. I didn't have a bean.

Richard opened accounts at the best stores and I could charge whatever I wanted. But no actual cash ever crossed my palm. I had to buy things in some stores sim-

ply to get my parking ticket validated. I could grandly
sign the bill in expensive restaurants, but I had no money
to buy the petrol to get me to them. When I was really
stuck I borrowed money from the butler.

To establish our arrival in Hollywood—and the big time
—Richard threw a huge party for me with a guest list of
350. A hundred came for dinner; the rest came at midnight for a champagne breakfast.

There were lots of names on the list that weren't familiar to me. By now I was getting used to that.

Richard had all the roses dyed lilac; a twenty-piece orchestra was hired, together with dozens of waiters, attendants, kitchen staff and security people.

The first guests arrived early. Richard had not returned
from the studio. I went downstairs to greet them, only to
discover that I didn't recognize any of them. I introduced
myself with all the charm and vivacity I could muster. I
was appalled to see that Eduardo had failed to offer them
a drink. I ordered him to do so at once. I greeted the next
arrival with similar animation and expressions of delight.
I told several complete strangers how much I had been
looking forward to meeting them and how very fond
Richard was of them. They seemed ill at ease; they began
to drift in an embarrassed fashion to the far end of the
room. Suddenly I noticed that one man had a violin in his
hand; another was fixing a mouthpiece to a trumpet.

I had been chatting up the band.

It was a lovely party. I danced a lot that evening with
Rex Harrison. I found I no longer felt remotely uncomfortable with him. Rachel was in high spirits. She quickly
got over her rage with Vanessa Redgrave, who had declined to sit next to Rex at dinner. (Rachel was always
protective of Rex's pre-eminence in Hollywood society.)
Having just fallen madly in love with Franco Nero,

Vanessa wanted to talk only to him and refused to budge from his side. Robert Mitchum was in the middle of a story (a yarn about the time he caught leprosy on the upper reaches of a minor tributary of the Congo) when a rousing look of pain came into his eyes. He looked slowly down. We all looked slowly down. Rachel was on her hands and knees giving a lifelike impersonation of a Welsh corgi. Having bitten clean through Mitchum's trousers, her teeth were now firmly planted in his leg. Mitchum was splendid. He patted her on the head, and continued his story.

Rachel confirmed her affinity with animals that night by opening the cage of a small African lovebird, releasing it into the night. She simply couldn't bear, she said, to see anything caged. Unfortunately, Richard had developed a reverent conviction that this bird had something to do with his own soul. He became frantic when he discovered the empty cage. I suggested it was probably taking some air and would return in due course. I planned to replace it the following morning. I couldn't find another African lovebird; I finally settled for a conveniently dumb Amazon parrot. Richard appeared not to notice the switch; although I don't think he ever quite trusted the parrot with his soul.

Rex and Rachel came into our lives rather a lot at that time. They were frequent guests at our parties and dinners, some of which were fairly intimate affairs for no more than fifty famous people. When these evenings got too boisterous, and guests, in various stages of undress, were taking to the pool, Rex became crotchety. He said to me one night, "Christ, Elizabeth, it's all such a bloody bore. I did all this years ago. What does Richard think he's doing in this house? Who is he trying to impress? It's so passé now. This is old Hollywood and old Hollywood is dead. You're twenty-five years too late."

A bore it was not.

There were nights when Richard and I would dine alone in that magnificent dining room, one at each end of the refectory table which ran down the room like a mahogany motorway. Candelabra flickered, romantic melodies were played in the shadows. Between each course, we would waltz around the room in sweeping sensual grandeur.

Those were the memorable moments. The beautiful mad moments when we became lovers again. The moments when we forgot all the bad things that had happened between us. But those moments soon faded and I knew again that I had to get away. Away from Richard, and away from Hollywood. I feared that I was losing touch with reality.

More and more I thought about Rex's remark: we *were* like ghosts haunting a Hollywood that had ceased to exist. Nothing was real. The house we lived in wasn't ours; my jewelry went back the next day; most of our new friends were mere acquaintances. Nobody talked about real issues or real problems; they talked about studio politics, percentages, scripts, package deals. It was pure *Alice in Wonderland*. The actor portraying the hero became more feted than the man he played. Oscars rate higher than Victoria Crosses. No one ever talked about the future, except in terms of the next role, the next production, the next marriage.

The real world is not always easy to live in, but there is nothing quite so unendurable as persistent unreality. I know now I was beginning to lose my reason.

One evening after a party Rex and Rachel gave at the Luau restaurant in Beverly Hills, Richard burst into one of his car-destroying rages. We were on our way home—I was driving—when he started to smash the interior of the Cadillac, cutting himself badly in the process. I remember feeling curiously apart from the mayhem about me; I continued to drive unhurriedly along Sunset Boulevard, observing the traffic lights and speed signs, as scrupulously as a Sunday driver. I was covered in his blood. I waited for the storm to subside. I didn't even feel enough contact with myself to stop the car and get out and run. I didn't feel fear or hatred or even curiosity. I felt . . . hopelessness, I suppose. I felt despair. I was soaked in his blood, it was on my clothes and in my hair; I could feel the soft warmth of it on my face, smelling of sulphur. I knew he was screaming but I heard nothing.

My breakdown came not because of the physical violence; finally it was my mind that couldn't cope, not my body. I didn't want to leave my room. I imagined spies everywhere. I felt and behaved like a prisoner. My telephone calls were monitored, everything I did was noted and reported to Richard. I took rooms apart looking for hidden tape recorders; I feigned sleep rather than get up and face the day.

Richard became my jailer, my inquisitor, my persecutor. Sometimes he would keep me awake all night cross-questioning me. He wanted to get inside my mind; never for one hour of the day or night could I relax. His suspicion was relentless, grinding, vindictive.

I'd crawl around my room; I felt safe crouched against the wall. I felt so small I wanted to cling to the floor; I felt safer on all fours. I had no real physical sense at all. The only feeling I had was in my head. I wasn't aware of my body any more. I had forgotten what I looked like. I wanted to flee. I felt I would smother to death if I couldn't get away. I didn't care if I ended up in one room in Bloomsbury, as long as it was mine and I didn't have to see anyone or answer to anyone or explain any more.

I recalled the first months of finishing school in Lausanne were an ordeal for me. I was afraid that I would be lured into Catholicism. All sorts of Roman plots, I imagined, were being hatched to lead me astray. For a long time I fought a private and totally imaginary holy war. I refused to attend church services; I declined to enter into any kind of religious debate; I resented being present when Grace was said before each meal. After a while I realized that nobody was greatly concerned about my Baptist beliefs. After getting over the shock at the absence of any conspiracy to convert me, I felt rather hurt. Abandoned. Was I not worth saving? My ego, if not my godliness, was roused. I started going to Mass and slipping into Benediction, hoping to encourage some interest in my soul. The nuns were courteous but displayed a stubborn indifference to my new theological vulnerability. Years later I realized that I had, in a fashion, been converted. I was a convert who lacked the courage, or perhaps the discipline, to take the final step. When I go to church now, which isn't very often, I go to Mass. I am glad that my sons have been raised as Catholics.

My time in Switzerland taught me an important lesson: I cannot be exposed to anything for very long without its getting to me in some way. I now feared Hollywood every bit as much as I once feared the convent in Lausanne. I wanted to see my children again; I wanted the familiarity of England. Richard finally agreed to let me go.

He came to the airport to see me off. I wanted him to go quickly. I was nervous in his presence. I longed to be on my own. The relief when I finally entered the plane was overwhelming. I slumped down, fastened the seat belt, and closed my eyes. I sensed someone take the seat beside me. I was too exhausted even to open my eyes to see what my traveling companion for the next twelve hours looked like. I was almost asleep when I heard a man's voice ask the steward for a drink. I went rigid. The person next to me was Richard.

I opened my eyes. He was staring at me, smiling.

I felt numb. I didn't know what to say.

He kept smiling at me, not moving.

It took several minutes to realize we were still on the ground.

"You can't come with me," I said. "You won't be allowed into England without your passport. They'll send you straight back."

He thought about this for a little while. I prayed that he didn't have his passport with him; he very seldom did.

"Yes," he said finally. "It's a long way to go just for a ride and free booze."

He finished his drink and stood up.

"I get off here," he told the steward.

I went with him to the exit. The last I saw of him as they closed the huge door was his eye staring at me through the peephole. I felt as if I had entered a padded cell. My feelings of relief disappeared. I didn't close my eyes once during that long polar flight to London.

The happiness and relief I felt at being with my sons again was short-lived. I had been in London only forty-eight hours when Pan Am telephoned. They were holding seats for us all to return to America on the weekend. Richard, they said, would be returning to collect us.

I couldn't face going back to Los Angeles; I knew that our marriage was over. I loved the Richard that had been —the poetic Richard, the wild Richard, the Richard who thought that swizzle sticks were imitation flowers. I was afraid of the man Richard had become. I called David Jacobs. He was a lawyer recommended to me by a ballet dancer I knew. I came straight to the point. I told him I wanted to divorce Richard and that I did not want to go back to Hollywood.

A smooth, experienced operator, Jacobs said he would get an injunction against Richard immediately. "He won't be able to contact you after that," he assured me. "There will be no way he can take the children out of the country without your approval or the court's permission." The case, he said, would be heard by a judge in chambers; there would be absolutely no publicity. After the injunction he would go to work on the divorce. I didn't know anything about Mr. Jacobs, except the evident impression he had made in ballet circles. I believed what he told me. I was told later that he relished publicity and specialized in the rather more scandalous litigations of show business. Also, he loved to be photographed with the stars and was always carefully made up for such occasions. In the circumstances, his promise that our case would receive no publicity was implausible. Mr. Jacobs went to the airport to serve the papers on Richard personally. But the press had been advised of his errand well in advance. The pictures of the confrontation duly made the front pages.

Richard understandably was hurt and for some time bitter about the way I had handled the affair. I didn't remain a client of Mr. Jacobs very long; he hanged himself in his garage not long after this, although this had no connection with my case.

I became reclusive. I felt inept, and insecure. It took a long while for me to recover my confidence. When I did, I discovered that I had changed.

During my years with Richard my alcoholic intake had dropped to nearly zero; I seldom took more than a

Babycham with dinner. Now I began to drink very heavily. There is a line in one of Richard's poems that says, "Run the length of your wildness." That is just what I did. I have never been very good at turning the other cheek. Now I couldn't rest until I had evened the score with Richard.

I behaved appallingly.

I had nine years to settle with him. And the next three years were spent doing exactly that.

I lied to him, I double-crossed him and I cheated. But I don't believe I ever really fooled him for one moment. How could I? He taught me everything I knew. After so many years of being responsible, I reveled in being irresponsible, in doing the things I had criticized Richard for doing. I stayed up for nights on end and slept the days away. I filled the house with people, only they were people of my choice now. I was extravagant, careless with money and profligate with the future.

My old nanny, Mrs. Beavil, had joined me in Bedford Gardens and the children's routine was unchanged. She made it quite clear that she did not approve of my liberated behavior. She belonged to the old school and I knew our days together were numbered. Still I was determined no longer to live the life other people wanted me to live: too bad if I didn't qualify for the Good Housekeeping Seal of Approval. I knew I had to find out what *I* wanted in life. I had gone from my father's house to my husband's bed at the age of twenty. I had no ungoverned experience. Now, very simply, I needed to sow my wild oats. It is not an activity to be recommended at such a late stage with three small children in tow. But I persevered. I had boy friends, and suitors too, but I was careful not to inflict on my sons a string of uncles. I took care they never saw their mother enjoying anything more than the most platonic friendship with the opposite sex.

Apart from Richard's absence, the most notable change in my life was the sudden lack of money. In a very short time I had become rather well acquainted with affluence. I had taken for granted chauffeurs and champagne, first-class travel, the best restaurants and the finest suites in the grandest hotels. Now little things like gas bills, electricity and telephone demands, rates, butchers' and grocers' accounts tended to be neglected. Although I had reduced my household staff and curtailed my tastes, it was not enough. I was always in debt. Money, or rather the lack of it, kept me constantly alert; I was always having to think up new schemes to extricate myself from some scrape or other. I never worried very much. I always expected something to turn up, and it usually did. If I'd been the sort of woman to worry about money and the future, I wouldn't have married a penniless actor in the first place. When the telephone was cut off, I simply installed another in another name. I didn't worry when we were deprived of electricity. The house looked pretty by candlelight, and we cooked by gas. Although I did find it unpleasant when they turned the water off. There really is no substitute for water.

London in the sixties had a reckless spirit of its own. There was a sparkle and a confidence about everyone I met. It was a decade of adventurers. We wanted to make our own mistakes and our own fortunes. Sexual freedom was new and exciting. We all felt very daring and very pleased with ourselves. I felt a great affinity with that time and place. The grand parties of Hollywood, the caviar and champagne and private orchestras had given way to spaghetti and Italian plonk and record players. But now I knew every name on the guest list and when I chatted up a musician I knew *exactly* what I was doing!

My Jaguar car sat motionless for months outside my house for want of petrol and insurance; writs arrived with monotonous regularity. An unfamiliar face at one of my amazingly frequent parties inquired whether I was Mrs. Harris. "Yes, but please call me Elizabeth and do have a drink."

"Thank you, Mrs. Harris," he said, slipping the familiar document into my hand, "and do have this writ."

Despite my difficulties, I managed to dress extraordinarily well; after a particularly successful meeting with the divorce lawyers—successful for Richard, that is—he had taken me to Cordoba's in Bond Street and spent £3,000 on leather outfits for me. "You made a ridiculous settlement," he said. "At least this lot will keep you warm." My friends were alarmed by my sudden penchant for leather. It gave quite the wrong impression.

I was now beginning to see a lot of Christopher Plummer. Born and brought up in Montreal, he had become a respected actor in the British theater and Hollywood movies. He was handsome and reserved, as undemanding as he was demonstrative. For a while I welcomed that, but I never felt I really knew him. He was never at ease with my sons. He developed an unfortunate habit of trying to entertain them whenever they met. "They always make me feel as if I have to audition for them," he grumbled. The children invariably stared at his performance with stony eyes. Had it been up to them I fear he may never have worked again.

In fact, ours was the sort of relationship that improved with distance. On transatlantic calls, he could be very affectionate, even quite intimate. Being together in the same room, alas, was never quite the same. But he did perform on the piano awfully well!

We became part of the Swinging London set, driving from fashionable first nights to fashionable restaurants to fashionable nightclubs in fashionable Rolls-Royce cars. We began to spend a lot of time with Rex and Rachel; she was good company. She could be warm, generous and wickedly amusing if her wit was aimed at somebody else. Chris's conservative nature did not permit total appreciation of her ribald asides; his dignity was sorely tested by being referred to as an old Colonial fart. She insisted she had never been known to leave a table while there was drink still on it. Maybe it was a Welsh superstition. One evening our cocktail hour at the Connaught had become extremely extended and we were late for a dinner appointment. Rachel eyed the remaining drinks and recited her dictum. "Never mind," she said. "We can soon remedy that." With undeniable panache she poured the remaining wine on to the floor. "There now," she said walking away triumphantly. "We can go."

"Christ," said Rex, remaining curiously aloof from the incident as if he were a bystander and not her husband. "Can't *somebody* do something about Rachel?"

A friend of mine, Janine Scott, had asked me if I could help her to get a premiere for the Zebra Trust, which was a charity organization helping African students studying in Britain. I told her that I would talk to Jack Warner about *Camelot*. We were finally given the first night, to share with another charity, Invalid Children's Aid Association, whose patron was Princess Margaret.

I was a member of the committee organizing the evening. As such, I was invited with forty other guests to a dinner given after the show at John St. Alban's town house in Knightsbridge. The guests of honor were Princess Margaret and Lord Snowdon. Richard, whom I had not seen for some time, was of course also invited as the star of the movie. He had brought over his sister Harmay and other members of his family from Ireland for the occasion. Chris escorted me.

It was to be a glamorous first night, and I needed a new dress. I had seen the most beautiful dress and cloak. The dress was of pale flowing green chiffon, its Empire line bodice encrusted with thousands of little pearls. It was very expensive and my funds were very low. After a quick look at my bank manager and my account, I realized I would have to find the solution elsewhere.

Many of the leather clothes Richard had earlier bought me for £3,000 at Cordoba's remained new or as good as new. Some of these I put into an auction and raised enough money for the dress, but not also the cloak.

My temperature rose every time I thought of all the disastrous possibilities that evening offered. It made me feel that the cloak would have been superfluous anyway.

The film was well received, all had gone smoothly and we drove to Knightsbridge. Richard and his family took up positions at one end of the room; Chris and I remained at the other. When dinner was announced, Chris was informed that Princess Margaret wished him to be seated on her left. I knew when I was outranked. On reaching the dining room, I saw, as I suspected, Richard was on her right.

Richard Kershaw, the TV interviewer, took me firmly by the arm. We were joined by Lord Snowdon, whom I had known in my deb days. Ivan Moffett, who said he knew everyone in London, made elaborate introductions. I wondered how the introductions were going at the top table. When Princess Margaret inquired whether Richard and Chris knew each other, Richard replied, "We share something in common."

After dinner Richard invited Chris and me back to his Chesham Place flat, where he was housing his relatives. The evening ended amicably enough, with all of us gathered around the piano while Chris played songs from *Camelot*.

For Christmas that year a group of us rented a large country house. Since I was the only one not working, I was put in charge of the arrangements. I found the perfect house, Harmere Hall in Sussex. Set in beautiful parkland, the Hall had large rooms with lofty ceilings, oak-paneling, uneven floors, mysterious corridors, creaking casement windows. It was the sort of house that Miss Havisham would have loved to haunt. Besides my maid, I hired a large waddling cook and a butler with a nervous twitch and faulty vision. The first evening at dinner he was so unnerved by an exploding champagne cork that several stiff brandies were required to steady him. He spilled a great deal of wine and ruined at least one beautiful gown that Christmas.

I loved that Christmas, but out of the dozen or so people who gathered at Harmere Hall, only Phil and Marie Rhodes were still together a year later. I don't know about the rest, but I certainly had a premonition that my days with Chris were numbered. On our last day in that lovely old house, Chris and I were standing with a farewell glass of champagne in our hands waiting for the transport to take us back to London.

After a while a gleaming fleet of Rolls-Royces were to be seen proceeding in a stately fashion up the long driveway.

Chris turned pale.

When he spoke his voice was small, as if it were coming from a great distance. Perhaps Montreal.

"You haven't ordered that lot simply to take us and the luggage back to London, have you?"

I nodded dumbly. I was aware that what was now creeping toward us was a funeral cortege. The hopes I had been harboring for a more permanent relationship with Mr. Plummer were dead.

I remembered too late: his contribution to the holiday was to pay for the transportation. Normally actors are particular about their traveling arrangements. Rex, for example, had a most commandeering attitude toward motorcars.

I recall vividly an occasion in Paris. It was the premiere of *A Flea in Her Ear* the Feydeau farce he had made with Rachel. It was a glittering occasion. Rex was making *Staircases* with Richard Burton at the time, and invited him and Elizabeth Taylor to be his personal guests. The Burtons at that time were at the height of their notoriety.

Although it was Rex and Rachel's evening, the Burtons attracted a great deal of attention, particularly the attention of the photographers. Rex's admirable indulgence of this situation, however, was finally exhausted. The climax came as we waited for our cars to take us to dinner at Maxim's. The photographers continued to besiege the Burtons. With angry aplomb, Rex swept the Burtons aside and, stepping into the waiting Rolls, declared loudly, "Fuck off, Burton. I'm bored with this vulgar display. I'm going."

A bemused Burton watched the Rolls glide silently away into the Paris night.

"I don't mind Rex telling me to fuck off," Burton said in a reasonable voice, "but I do wish he'd stop taking my Rolls."

Warren Beatty came to our rescue with *his* Rolls.

9. *Mrs. R.H.—Again*

Life has a habit of repeating itself, I thought. Joan Thring and I were weaving our way along the Promenade des Anglais in Nice, munching hard-boiled eggs in the little red Renault. We had just left one millionaire's home, Rudolf Nureyev's, in the clouds above Le Turbe, and were on our way to stay with another millionaire, Tommy Kayle, in Cannes. We couldn't afford to buy lunch *and* tip the servants. Hence the hard-boiled eggs. It reminded me of my debutante days when I had been taken by wealthy young men to the Café de Paris, the Milroy or the 400; my problem then had been stretching my £2-a-week allowance to cover lunches at RADA, fares, clothes, makeup, and—most important of all—tips for attendants in the ladies' room.

I had been in London barely twenty-four hours from the South of France when my brother Morgan invited me to go with him and Sir William Piggott Brown to California for a week. Morgan and William had recently launched a theatrical agency and were hoping to sign up Richard.

Richard entertained us royally but turned them down. To cheer them up I suggested we come home via Nassau and spend a few days in the sun.

We arrived in a Sadie Thompson rainstorm. After a few telephone calls, William learned that it was gloriously sunny in Jamaica and that Golden Eye, the house where Ian Fleming had written his Bond books, was at our disposal for ten days. I loved it there. I found it hard to believe that I was so debt-ridden.

We returned to London via New York, where we had a twelve-hour stopover. I was kicking my heels, wondering what to do, wishing I had money, when I remembered I had the next-best thing. Richard's account at Saks Fifth Avenue. I was, after all, however precariously, still Mrs. Richard Harris.

I hastened across town and ran through Saks like a wild thing. Eschewing elevators, taking the stairs three at a time, I managed to purchase an impressive array of coats, dresses, suits and shoes. A few weeks later when Richard turned up to buy his latest lady some finery, he was informed that the manager was anxious to meet him. Richard was pleased that his patronage merited such attention. It wasn't until they handed him a large bill that he got the message. His accounts with several London stores where I had also given my patronage generously (especially to those establishments sporting wine departments) were closed at once.

By the time he returned to London, all was more or less forgiven, if not paid for. He rented a garden flat in Chesham Place. I fell into the habit of dropping in. It was a habit that unnerved Richard quite a bit, not to mention the ladies he may have been entertaining.

Late one evening I arrived in a state of considerable tiredness. I had been drinking heavily at lunch with a convivial crowd at the White Elephant. Luncheon had somehow spilled over into the cocktail hour, and the cocktail hour had lasted right through dinner.

"I feel like a little nightcap," I announced defiantly. Richard was apprehensive but agreed to pour me a glass of champagne. He listened to my ramblings with that amused tolerance that the very sober reserve for the very drunk.

Finally he announced that it was past his bedtime and left the room.

I didn't feel like going home. I put on some music and poured myself another drink. It was very late and after a while I decided I would stay the night. I went to the bathroom and found some sleeping tablets; I took them with another drink. I didn't feel tired at all. I decided the answer was more sleeping tablets. Had I taken two? Or four? Had I taken any? I was bemused. Tyrannosaurus Rex and Bob Dylan merged and separated and merged again. . . .

My throat ached. My mouth tasted foully of salt. After a few minutes I recognized one of the faces staring down at me.

"Christ, it's that fucking quack Snavely," I said.

"She recognizes me," I heard Dr. Snavely murmur humbly. "She is going to be fine."

I recognized Richard. There were several other people around the bed. People I didn't know, or couldn't make out. They were all talking in those anxious undertones people always use when talking about the very sick, or the dying. I concentrated very hard, trying to understand what they were saying. I tried to swallow but the pain in my throat was so bad I couldn't. My stomach had been pumped.

"I don't want her to stay here," Richard said to somebody.

"She must have medical supervision . . . she really shouldn't be moved . . ." said Snavely.

I realized now I was in a hospital.

"I have to go home," I said.

Richard agreed to hire a day and night nurse to look after me in Chesham Place; he dispatched an aide to prepare the flat for my arrival. When we got to Chesham Place we discovered the aide in a moaning heap at the foot of the stairs; in his eagerness to carry out Richard's orders, he had tripped over a mat and sprained his ankle.

Richard never complained about the trouble I had caused. He had found me just in time, he said. He had returned to the living room for a book . . .

After a couple of days I was pronounced well again. Richard had his cook prepare dinner for two. The dining room was softly lit by candles, a big fire burned in the hearth. I can't remember what started it, but before the cook had time to present her prized *zabaione* I was out on the street.

I didn't see Richard for several months.

Not until I saw my children again did the full horror of what had happened hit me. It was an accident ("death by misadventure" would have been the probable verdict with all its innuendo), but the children could never have been really sure. I decided it was time to do something about my drinking.

I continued to try various methods of boosting my ever-sinking finances. A stab at interior decorating was no more successful than my venture into costume design. Both ended up costing me money in some extraordinary fashion. Then I had a shot at modeling. My first assignment was for a health product. On the day of the session,

I was indisposed. I inquired whether it was possible for the photographer to come to me. It was unusual, he said, but since it was a comparatively simple head shot it could be arranged. I gave him the address: 20 Devonshire Place, W1.

"Do you live here?" he asked, a bit puzzled.

"Not exactly," I answered evasively.

"I've never been here before," he said. "The London Clinic."

"Really?" I said. I tried to sound a bit dim. Our location was a subject I wasn't immensely keen to pursue. His assistant was making a lot of fuss setting up the lights in the front hall. I went through my paces; the photographer snapped away. I was pleased to see the back of him and his paraphernalia; the hall porters were beginning to look suspicious. I went quickly upstairs to my room, undressed and returned to bed.

"You can't take chances with pleurisy," the nurse told me. My temperature had risen several degrees. She couldn't understand it. My face did become quite famous on the Northern Line, advertising tonic wine.

After three years of fights and reconciliations, Richard and I were divorced at 3:45 in the afternoon of July 25, 1969. At last I could begin to rebuild my life.

I rented a lovely old house in Wiltshire with my friend Susy Coe. We took our children there to spend what was left of the late summer. There were plenty of things to amuse the children. There were ponies, a swimming pool, tennis courts and deep woods to ramble through. I lazed around, reading more than I had read in the past nine years put together. It was good to relax into the slow country pace after all those hectic times in London. Susy and I enjoyed sitting outside the old stone village pub, nursing our half pints of cider before lunch. I felt at peace with the world and with Richard.

During those weeks I tried to put my life into some sort of perspective. I decided that the theater was not, after all, the world for me. Actors were not for me. They could be amusing and often exciting, too . . . but they were simply not my kind of men. I didn't feel that a wife was much of an asset to an actor. I wanted to contribute to a partnership, not compete; and I didn't want to be forever waiting in the wings.

I was not unduly worried about the future; something was bound to happen. I gained a kind of comfort from the countryside around me. Perhaps I identified with the autumn insects! Autumn insects seem to be more clumsy than the summer kind. The autumn fly flails and crashes around your bedroom; the autumn wasp collapses into hidden places and stings by accident and out of fear.

I returned to London in late September to find a letter waiting for me from Rachel. It was the first I had heard from the Harrisons since our holiday together. They had invited me to join them on the *Calisto*, the yacht Rex had chartered. He had also invited his agent, Lawrence Evans, and his wife Mary. With an eleven-man crew to look after the five of us, we had sailed in great style around the islands of Sardinia, Elba and Corsica. I left the yacht in Naples and flew to Madrid, where I joined up with some old friends. I pleasurably recalled that time as I read Rachel's note. She was returning to England to begin a tour of *Who's Afraid of Virginia Woolf?* with her ex-husband Alan Dobie. Rex, she said, was also coming back to London to start rehearsals for a new play called *The Lionel Touch*.

I wondered again about the state of their marriage. I knew that Rex was disappointed that filming together in

Paris on *A Flea in Her Ear* had not strengthened their relationship. I was never certain how serious their fights were. I had seen them together at times when they were both obviously unhappy and not very loving toward each other. Equally I had seen them together—like the time we spent on the *Calisto*—when they looked happy and appeared to be in love. I never took seriously Rachel's claims, usually made in front of Rex, that they were getting divorced. I know that Rachel was anxious to resume her career. I knew that from time to time she had taken a flat on her own.

When Rachel began her tour of *Virginia Woolf*, Rex, alone in London, would often call on me unannounced at my home in Bedford Gardens. I was pleased with his informal visits; it was that sort of house. At that time I had a composer named Kathy Green staying with me; she was working on her first album. My small living room was now bulging with a grand piano, and guests had a choice of sitting on it or under it. The place began to resemble a musicians' drinking club. Kathy felt at her composing best at 5 A.M. Her nocturnal rhapsodies were not appreciated by the neighbors. "Holy Christ," complained one irate gentleman coming to my door in his dressing gown at dawn, "I've heard that lousy song fifty times. I hate it." I pointed out that he was in a privileged position as the first member of the public to have heard it.

"The pianist," I confided, "is also the composer."

"Then shoot the bloody pianist," he said rudely. I didn't realize at the time what a discerning critic he was.

In this atmosphere of casual chaos Rex took pot luck with the rest of us. The food, without fail, was awful; the champagne, when there was any, definitely non-vintage. It was hardly the life style he was used to.

I could see that he was intensely lonely; but he isn't a

man who can talk freely about his feelings and I had no idea just how unhappy he was. My house was a comfortable noisy refuge where he could, for a moment, forget his troubles. I found Rex enormously attractive. He enjoys women's company, and his charm, at times, can be overwhelming. I noticed that very few women were unaware of his presence. He had a delightful vagueness. Later I learned it was a single-mindedness that set him apart from anyone I had ever met. It is a necessary quality if an actor is to become and remain an international star for three decades.

Gradually he began to confide in me. We spent hours talking together; I remembered with amazement the time when I felt so ill at ease with him. Now he was so open with me; he seemed so very vulnerable. One evening he said to me, "If you could be born again, what is the one thing you would ask for?"

I said, "A sense of humor."

He said, "And I would ask not to be so damned dependent on women."

He and Rachel were separated now, although not officially. Neither seemed to know what they really wanted. One evening I got a telephone call from Rachel. She came immediately to the point.

"What's all this then I heard about you and Rex?"

I said, "I don't know, Rachel. Tell me what you're hearing."

"You and Rex," she said, "are seeing a lot of each other."

I said that was true.

"Are you in love with him?"

After a long pause I said, "Yes, I am."

This time the long pause was hers. Quietly she thanked me for telling her the truth. I felt terrible. It would have been a lot easier if I hadn't liked Rachel, but I did. I told her I was sorry I had fallen in love with Rex.

"It happens," she said. Her voice was so flat now, without accusation, without malice. I didn't know what to say to her. I hadn't wanted to fall in love with Rex. It had happened slowly, almost without my noticing. It was all a hideous muddle. There were no adequate excuses. She was my friend and I had fallen in love with her husband.

A few evenings later I had gone to bed early, having taken two sleeping pills. Rex, who had spent the evening with me, was on his way out when he saw Rachel coming up the path. He returned and came to my bedroom and told me to get dressed quickly. "You can't receive her in that negligee," he said impatiently. "Come on, do hurry." I obediently dressed and descended the stairs very unsteadily, one of the reasons being the Mandrax, which was now beginning to work very effectively.

It was a bizarre scene.

Jamie's small dog Dodger was jumping excitedly around my feet as I tried, very shakily, to pour Rex and Rachel a drink. They stood around like guests who have arrived too early for a party. Finally Rachel spoke.

"All right, Rex. Make up your mind. Which one of us do you want? You must make a choice. Now."

Rex took a long desperate look at each of us in turn. Then he pointed to the dog. "I'll take Dodger," he said, and was out of the house like hell on stilts.

Rachel and I were left staring blankly at each other.

The Mandrax had by now taken over. I was sagging badly at the knees. Rachel feared that I was about to faint clean away from the sheer emotion of it all.

"Go to bed, love, before you fall down," she said kindly. "Can you make it up the stairs?"

I nodded.

"I'll let myself out," she said. "It's been a funny old night, hasn't it?"

Rex was having problems with the play; lines were being changed nightly. He also had his work cut out keeping up with the scene changes in his private life. The strain on him was considerable. His doctor, a rather nice, rather old-fashioned Scottish gentleman, finally ordered him to take a complete rest. He left the play for three weeks.

Rex and Rachel's lawyers now had their heads together and their separation took on a more permanent look. Rachel took off for Los Angeles, where she had been offered a movie.

Rex could be as extravagant as anyone when he wanted to be. The night *The Lionel Touch* closed in London, we drove straight to Luton Airport and boarded a private jetliner to Tangier, where the *Calisto* was waiting for us. There was a clandestine atmosphere about our midnight embarkation. The press was now becoming inquisitive. Rex suggested that we invite a few friends along. I thought that was a splendid idea. I also took along Jamie and his nanny. Damian and Jared were at their prep school.

After ten days, Jamie, nanny and our friends returned to England. For the first time Rex and I were on our own. Free from lawyers, agents, public relations people, the press. We were like small children suddenly let out of school. Rex suggested we sail in search of the most remote island we could find. The captain suggested the island of Lanzarote, a tiny Spanish outpost several hundred miles off the west coast of Morocco. After several days of rough sailing we got there. We knew at once why it was so little visited. It was barren, boring and very primitive.

Rex cabled his secretary to send a plane to get us out of there quickly. She dispatched the largest private jetliner I have ever seen. We flew to Fez, then drove through the Atlas Mountains to Agadir, where the *Calisto* was waiting for us.

Rex was impressed with Fez, the country's cultural and intellectual capital; he suggested we stay a few days. We booked into the Palais Jamai, a beautiful hotel built at the end of the nineteenth century and based on a seventeenth-century palace of exquisite splendor. Rex was greeted like a prince: an assistant manager was appointed to act as our personal guide to the city and the night life.

By the time we reached the third or fourth nightclub, I was in a sociable mood and keen to dance. Rex whirled me around the small dance floor a couple of times, then insisted on returning to his conversation with the well-informed assistant manager. The fact that Fez was founded as Morocco's first political capital in the ninth century by the son of a refugee Arab prince from Baghdad wasn't exactly my idea of cozy nightclub intercourse. Rex appeared to be utterly engrossed in the political development of the city. Perhaps it was a ruse to avoid dancing with me; my style was dangerously energetic. I can see that now.

A handsome young Arab with the kind of good looks that suggest the shadiest antecedents had noticed Rex's neglect. He invited me to join him on the dance floor. I accepted gratefully. It was a mistake. He was an agile fellow and clearly a lovely mover. He saw Rex's fist swinging toward him. Like a shadow, he ducked and was gone. I caught the blow smack on the chin and went down for the count as if poleaxed.

"Darling Elizabeth." Rex was bending over me. A small crowd had gathered, looking down at the tableau. My jaw felt like a balloon. "Poor Elizabeth, darling Elizabeth, are you all right?"

"I think so."

"How awful, darling." Through the enveloping fog I now recognized the anger as well as the concern in his voice. "It was a terrible thing to have done."

"It's all right, Rex. It was an accident," I reassured him. I was embarrassed by the presence of the general public, and now a regiment of the lesser servitors from the kitchen had joined the throng around us.

"It was no accident. That bloody little Arab did it on purpose," Rex said. He was very cross. I was confused.

"He could see perfectly well that I intended to bean *him* and he bloody well ducked," Rex explained. "Of course he did it on purpose. He *made* me miss."

Rex always had his own curious rationalization of facts and events. He never could understand my reluctance, for example, to let him drive us to Agadir over the Atlas Mountains after our sojourn in Fez. He believed that being blind in one eye was sufficiently compensated for by having double vision in the other eye. "It doesn't affect my driving skills one bit," he insisted. I said it affected my courage more than a bit; I persuaded him to let me drive to Agadir. He grumbled all the way.

I wanted to thank Rex for his hospitality. I suggested I give him a birthday party in London. Oddly enough, he was very much against the idea. He became vehement on the subject. I was puzzled for a time; Rex adores people to remember his birthday; he loves to be made a fuss of; he plans the event weeks ahead.

I finally discovered the problem: Rachel had promised to give him a birthday party in Los Angeles. When he at last confessed his dilemma, I told him there was a very simple answer.

"What's that?" he asked suspiciously.

"You must have an official birthday as well as a private birthday. All the top people do it."

As a man who modestly called his autobiography *Rex*, he found the idea immensely appealing.

Most of that summer was spent on chartered yachts, or at Rex's villa in Portofino.

I found life at Portofino difficult. I never felt at home there. I felt like something between an intruder and an unexpected guest.

The house seemed to be full of ghosts. Occasionally, Rex would get my name wrong there, a thing he never did anywhere else in the world. Once when I arrived after a particularly tiring journey, I tried a feeble joke: "All right, Rex. Which wife is staying with us this time?"

He didn't smile. He said wearily, "The trouble is, they're all here."

I set the table that evening. I carefully laid five places. . . . He didn't think it was very amusing.

The servants had been trained by the servants who had been there in Lilli Palmer's time, and everything went on in much the same way as it always had. It was a beautiful house, with breathtaking views. But more than anything else, it was a house with a sense of *déjà vu*, which I didn't like at all.

Richard had had the children barred by the courts from visiting Portofino, despite my pleas that we planned to marry as soon as Rex was free to do so. Rex rented a summer house in Le Lavandou in the South of France. The children always invited their cousins and friends on holiday. This year was no exception. At one time there were twenty-two of us in the house, including students from Edinburgh University engaged to look after the eleven kids.

I thought that Rex would enjoy the spontaneity and informality that goes with living with so many young people. There was always music, in a variety of tastes, usually being played at the same time. It was a noisy, funny, confusing time. Particularly confusing for the local doctor. He found it simpler, with so many children to keep an eye on, to hold surgery twice a week at the house. There were the usual summer colds, grazed knees and upset stomachs to treat. After a few visits, Rex asked him for vitamin injections. Under the impression that Rex was the father of the brood he was treating, the doctor was bemused by this request. Rex never understood his strange looks.

Many of my friends came down that year, bringing their families. Maria St. Just, Richard Kershaw, Clair Deutsch and Father Tom. Rex's son Carey also visited us. Life was very much like it had been in Bedford Gardens. Only now Rex didn't seem to enjoy it so much. This time the chaos was not contented. Rex missed the routine of quiet drinks before lunch and dinner; his vodka and tonics became more of a need then an appetizer. It was not a particularly happy holiday for Rex. His customary preoccupation with himself became more marked than ever. When Father Tom arrived, Rex promptly ordered him to use his influence with the Almighty to heal him of a nagging minor discomfort. "I want you to say a prayer to relieve me," he said, coming straight to the point. Father Tom said he would do his best but offhand knew of no supplication that covered that particular emergency. I could see that Rex felt personally let down by this omission in the Church's repertoire.

That holiday very nearly finished off our romance forever. I returned to London with the children. I suggested to Rex that he go back to Portofino to think things over. He agreed with alarming alacrity.

Two days after my return to Bedford Gardens, I got a call from Rex. He sounded distraught. "I can't stand it," he said. "All this silence. I can't cope with it any more. I miss you madly and I even miss all those buggering kids."

Rex returned to London and took a flat on Eaton Square. He started the television production of *Platinov*. I spent my time between his apartment and Bedford Gardens. It was not an ideal arrangement. I cannot pretend our courtship was calm. We were both very jealous of each other; we were unreasonably possessive. What was worse, we both had "pasts" that kept cropping up. It really was quite ridiculous. There was no way that people of our age could not have had a crowded life. For some reason we found that difficult to accept. We were being very childish. When you are in love, you are not always at your logical best.

The fact is, Rex and I were still recovering from our old heartaches. We were both vulnerable. We really met too soon; there had been no time to become whole again. But by now we had become committed to each other and to our plan to wed.

We discussed possible venues for the ceremony. America seemed the best bet. Rex said he'd had registry offices, and the Church had had us. We arrived in New York a week ahead of the wedding day in order to take and hopefully pass our Wassermann tests.

On our wedding eve we dined with a few friends at our favorite New York restaurant, the "21." Rex began musing in a lordly way over the large and splendid wine list. He takes his wine very seriously and hates to be interrupted while studying the *carte des vins*. The last time we dined at the "21" he was in the middle of debating with himself between the Château Mouton-Rothschild 1945 and a Château Haut-Brion 1955 when a lean handsome man came to our table and asked to shake Rex's hand.

"It really is my day," he had said. "We've come in on the last flight. You've given me so much pleasure through the years, Mr. Harrison, I would like to take this opportunity to thank you."

Rex bowed his head graciously, his expression bland, all his surfaces suave. It was apparent where Rex's keenest interest lay; he returned his attention to the wine list as soon as the American had gone.

Rex's admirer was part of a large group celebrating at a table decorated with dozens of miniature Stars and Stripes; they were all much fussed over by the waiters and obviously the center of considerable admiration, like people caught in a stage spotlight. Rex appeared not to notice any of this. Later, when the people at this table got up to leave, the same handsome American returned to our table and again said that after coming in on the last flight he was truly delighted to have met Rex.

"What a very odd fellow," Rex said when the American had finally gone. "I don't know why he should have made such a fuss about *his* last flight. I came in on the last flight from London. I don't go on and on about it, do I?"

"Rex," I pointed out gently. "That was James Lovell. He's just got back from the moon."

We were married at Alan Jay Lerner's beautiful Georgian house on Long Island. Alan had arranged everything; he had transformed his blue-and-white dining room into the most romantic of wedding parlors, overflowing with white flowers. A buffet with every imaginable exotic delicacy was laid out on the wide marble terrace above the green lawns that sloped down to the water's edge. Alan's style and taste is reflected in all he does. Having met him, I realized that the elegance of *Gigi* and *My Fair Lady* was an extension of the man. This air of timeless poise, the last word in civilized celebration, had only one uncomfortable aspect. The bride almost ruined the whole thing.

To help calm my nerves, I had slipped a Valium under my tongue. In the excitement I had not looked very carefully at the label on the bottle; it was only when the judge was nearing the end of the service that I became acutely aware of my mistake. Instead of a Valium, I had taken a diet pill—a pill to make me pee. I managed to contain myself long enough to hear the judge pronounce us man and wife.

Rex looked so handsome and happy that day. I was proud of him and proud to be his wife. I believed we had both learned a lot from our past mistakes. We knew all the pitfalls; I at least was sure that I would be able to avoid them the second time around.

We took a lovely house in Wilton Crescent, Belgravia, a large, elegant town house with a lift making light work of the six floors. The beautiful pine-paneled drawing room on the first floor led out onto a roof garden. In the morning we would hear the horses on their way to Hyde Park. It was a vast house, certainly the biggest we had ever taken, and needed an army of servants. On our return we gave a wedding party for about three hundred guests. I don't think that Rex's sisters were too thrilled that their younger brother had walked up the aisle again. In a world where a second marriage is considered indiscreet, a fifth fling is positively informal. His sister Sylvia, now Countess of Delawar, left me in no doubt as to her views. "Oh my God," she gasped after we had exchanged some fairly forthright opinions on the subject, "Rex does pick them!"

Nevertheless, Rex and I settled into a state of happy and promising domesticity. His years in the theater had left him with a heightened sense of timing; he lectured me often on the importance of promptness. He meticulously and at once organized a timetable for all our meals. This, in the beginning at least, was a welcome change from Richard's harum-scarum ways and erratic regard for mealtimes; he would disappear for a quiet drink before dinner and not return for several weeks. He had fancied a quiet drink in Dublin, he might explain—even though we were living in London at the time.

Rex, too, had his little idiosyncrasies. Now that we were married I naturally assumed I would take over as mistress of the house. I had noted his autocratic behavior in Portofino, where he dominated the entire household; I simply supposed this magisterial manner was necessitated by the disturbing turnover in the matrimonial arrangements. I was taken aback to find many of my most modest housewifery whims questioned and revoked. I ordered daffodils for the window boxes; Rex changed the order to wallflowers. "Wallflowers," he said, "last longer."

His sublime stamp on the household was total and emphatic. He was bound in his accustomed style; he was too set in his ways to respond to anything spontaneous. Even a simple picnic became an affair of complicated logistics and advance planning.

On a visit to the racecourse with my cousin Margaret and our children, we tucked gleefully into sandwiches, potato crisps and cider on the grass; Rex remained in solitary splendor in the back of his Phantom V, lunching from a table laden with Wedgwood, damask, Waterford and Georgian silverware, his chauffeur delicately producing an amazing variety of meats and fishes, beautifully displayed on a carriage table, for Rex's approval. He sipped pleasantly at a Bâtard-Montrachet 1957 as he followed the races on a portable television installed in the car. "I had no idea picnics could be so much fun," he assured me afterward. The only moment of ruffled tranquillity for Rex came at the end of the day when he was required to stand in line to collect the children's winnings at the 20p window. Rex in line for anything—let alone such bagatelle—is an incongruous sight.

At Ascot, he was called upon to suffer no such indignities. We took a box for the Royal Week. He enjoyed being back in the English scene after such a long absence; I rather think the English scene looked complete again.

We never stayed in any country for long. I was soon looking forward to our visit to Germany and particularly to East Berlin, a part of the world I had never visited before. Rex had been told it was advisable to call the British Consulate and acquaint them of our plans to go through Check Point Charlie. I heard him talking to the Consulate several times, making sure they fully understood the arrangements. He told them he would call the moment he got back to put their minds at rest. I don't know if some sinister plot had gone amiss but neither my name nor my presence on the excursion was ever mentioned in any of his conversations. I was not only pleased to get back, I was thankful.

Besides the lack of *joie de vivre* in East Berlin, the food left much to be desired. As I had been traveling extensively around the world, I had decided to put each country to a simple culinary test: I always ordered a Welsh rarebit. East Berlin came bottom of the league; Malaya came out on top. I am still not sure what conclusions to draw from this.

I soon discovered that Rex's conservatism had some surprising and endearing loopholes. When I told him I had never been to a red-light district in my life he was aghast. No lady's education was complete, he said, without treading the red-light fantastic at least once. He quickly and knowingly arranged to take me to Amsterdam, a city I had always associated with tulips. I dressed carefully, and with a certain protective primness. I wore a long white woolen suit over a white high-necked Victorian blouse. I brushed my long hair back and wore it hanging loosely, kept in place with a small white ribbon. Rex wasn't too pleased with my appearance, particularly when the taxi driver told him that he had no right to be taking such a proper lady to such an improper place.

It was more picturesque than I expected. The streets were well lit, cobbled and narrow; the ladies sat in lighted windows, the tools of their trade discreetly displayed in the background. While I suppose it was not exactly good clean fun, it didn't look exactly evil either. I found it more carnival than carnal. It was soon apparent to me that I was in no danger.

Perhaps I looked in particular need of help; perhaps the taxi driver had put the finger on me; or maybe my virginal millinery had something to do with it . . . but every step we took was dogged.

Hymn-singing, tambourine-bashing, drum-beating soldiers of the Salvation Army pursued us everywhere. When we came to a small theater advertising the kind of adult divertissement that Lord Longford is concerned with (since he had displayed such a keen interest in my concerns when I married Richard, I felt the least I could do was to show some concern for his interests), the soldiers took up attacking positions and fired all their hallelujah fervor at us. We retreated. They may have saved our souls, but they didn't half bugger up our desires.

Although he was happy to tour the whorehouses of Amsterdam with his new bride, Rex's sense of privacy could occasionally be cranky. The lengths he would go to ensure his seclusion were sometimes inordinate. He had a dread of being ensnared into appearing on "This Is Your Life." This was particularly embarrassing to me since Eamonn Andrews, the compere of the show in England, was an old friend of mine. Every time he appeared at the house, Rex developed a suspicious, haunted look.

No assurances from me that I would never be a party to any conspiracy to lure him onto that show could set Rex's mind at rest. He continued to treat Eamonn with the utmost misgiving.

When Eamonn invited us to a surprise twenty-first wedding anniversary party for his wife Grainner at Foo Tong's restaurant in Kensington, Rex believed the very worst.

"If Andrews walks in with that stupid book under his arm, I'll hit him with it," he warned me. I promised him nothing of the kind would happen. It was a private party for a dozen friends.

That night Rex was unbelievably rude to Eamonn. It was Rex at his most arrogant. I was very upset. "I don't think Eamonn will ever speak to us again. Your behavior was unforgivable," I said when we got home.

The look of deliverance in Rex's eyes was unmistakable.

Our life at Wilton Crescent soon had a sense of remoteness about it. Geographically situated in the heart of London, I felt as far removed from my friends and the life I had known as I had once felt in Earls Court Road above the underwear shop. I appeared to be surrounded by a wall of servants.

Our routine was rigid to the nth degree. Ice had to be placed in the three bars at 11:45 A.M. and 5:45 P.M. The regular three-course lunch was at 1 P.M. sharp; dinner at 8 P.M. I eventually persuaded Rex to lunch without me. I found the enormous dining room at lunchtime depressingly formal. Often all I wanted was a cheese sandwich. Rex adored his food and regarded any sign of culinary informality as brutish if not barbarous. The butler stood behind him as he ate in solitary solemnity.

10. *Rex the Relentless Star*

Gerald Savory, then head of television plays at the BBC
and responsible for such successes as *Henry VIII* and
Elizabeth I, asked Rex to play Don Quixote in a BBC
coproduction with Universal. Rex was nervous of television but respected Gerald's judgment and was impressed
with his enthusiasm for the project. Quixote was also exactly the sort of challenge Rex was looking for at that
time.

Location filming was done on the plains of La Mancha,
also known as the frying pan of Spain. It was a place sensible travelers passed through as quickly as possible; we
were there for two months.

It has been said that from *Don Quixote* we get a better
idea of life in Spain three hundred years ago than any history book could give us. I quite believe it now. The primitive squalor of some of the villages in which we filmed,
with all their old ways and manners still intact, made for
a realistic if uncomfortable production. One village in
which we stayed had once known the miracle of elec-

tricity but the man who dealt with it had died and nobody bothered with it after that.

Sheila Brennan, Gerald Savory's wife, and I became firm friends; we kept each other amused—if not always out of trouble—during the long hot hours when our husbands and everyone else were so busy on the production.

One afternoon we persuaded the village mayoress, a large unquenchable female who was also the neighborhood barmaid, to introduce us to the joys of the local vino. She poured it from a gin bottle, assuring us it was none of your *ordinaire* rubbish, but the finest wine we would ever taste in the whole of La Mancha. Her husband, the mayor, barber and Coca-Cola representative, swore by it.

We went in search of our husbands to tell them of our amazing discovery. We can still be seen, two very shaky twentieth-century ladies, in a long shot of Don Quixote returning from some seventeenth-century affray.

I am never less than awed by Rex whenever I watch him work. His dedication is total; he drives himself as well as others mercilessly. During the whole time we were in La Mancha he was in considerable pain. He had broken three ribs in a fall a few weeks before in Portofino. He could now only get out of bed each morning by first rolling onto the floor, then pulling himself up to a kneeling position, and finally easing himself upright.

The roads were abominable, often little more than cart tracks, and the Spanish appeared to believe that suspension was something in a Hitchcock movie. Even with his ribs carefully strapped, a ninety-minute journey to the location would take Rex nearly twice as long. He had to mount his horse by means of a stepladder; he would remain in the saddle for hours since it was too painful to dismount between takes. A man was employed to stand at the top of the steps with a large umbrella to protect him from the horseflies and the sun. It was an unusual sight.

Back at the studio, Rex regained some of his old poise. Dissatisfied with the canteen food, he ordered our chef to prepare him luncheon every day; this had to be transported to the studio in the Rolls at noon precisely. Manuelle, the butler, went with it, as did the usual inventory of linen, china, glass and silverware. Luncheon was served in Rex's dressing room, usually with a perfectly chilled bottle of Montrachet '64 Marquis de Laguiche. Manuelle would discreetly withdraw to the corridor until summoned to replenish glass or plate. Rex is the only man I know who can become as absorbed in a meal as some men become absorbed in a good book.

At the end of 1972, Rex flew to New York to begin rehearsals for Pirandello's *Henry IV*. I followed a few weeks later with the children and their nanny, Rena, who was a colleen from Waterford. The boys were very fond of her. She had a marvelous direct way with them. If they needed to be reprimanded she would simply shout, "Come here now, while I thump you."

Unable to get away from rehearsals, Rex had organized a public relations man to meet us.

"I've given him a complete description of you," Rex assured me on the telephone. "He'll steer you through customs and the immigration rigmarole." I was thankful for that.

I arrived at Kennedy covered from top to toe in silver fox (the winter was mild but the furs were new). The P.R. man spotted us at once and advanced on us with a big welcoming smile. He advanced right past me and shook Rena warmly by the hand. "Welcome to New York City, Mrs. Harrison," he said with great sincerity. "I recognized you at once. Couldn't miss you after your husband's graphic description."

I could never see it myself, but the boys had often commented on the resemblance between Rachel and Rena. I could only imagine that Rex had suffered a temporary time lapse when describing his wife.

Certainly Rex had a great deal on his mind. He was very nervous about undertaking the Pirandello play; a play about insanity, real and faked. Rex was to portray a 1920s Roman millionaire who appears to believe himself to be the eleventh-century Emperor, a tyrant of enormous charm and menacing temper. Because of his great riches, he is able to sustain the mad fantasy, surrounding himself with a court of sycophants and parasites, all paid to act out their groveling loyalty. It is a massive, complex part and a formidable challenge to any actor, even to one of Rex's considerable talent. I knew that it often made him physically sick with fear and apprehension. It amazed me. He could have chosen almost any play he wanted; Sol Hurok, the Broadway impresario, would most certainly have backed him. Yet he drove himself to play the Emperor Henry. It was not a typical Harrison vehicle. It was alien to anything he had ever done in his whole career. Moreover, it was a little-performed play with an uncertain appeal to modern audiences. Rex knew perfectly well the risk he was taking. I could see the strain growing deeper in his face every day. Again I wondered, as I had wondered years before in Hollywood while watching the dying Gary Cooper pushing himself to the limits, what it is that drives an actor to such lengths.

Rex's daily routine began at 6 A.M. He would rise, bathe and withdraw immediately into the sitting room of our Waldorf Towers suite, forty-four floors above Park Avenue, to study his lines. Breakfast was at 8:30. Rehearsals started one hour later. He returned at 6 P.M. and spent the next two hours unwinding with me and the children. Dinner was at 8:30 and we usually dined alone in the suite; it was never a lingering affair, since he liked to spend an hour on the script before retiring at 10:30.

It was not a very happy holiday for the children; the tension in the suite was unrelieved, although Rex did make an effort to slip into the Christmas spirit on the day. He came to Mass with us at St. Patrick's Cathedral on Christmas morning. He appeared to be praying very hard; I presumed it was about the play.

Later in the day, his first wife, Collette, paid us a visit and confused the children by asking, "Do you mind, Elizabeth, if I kiss my husband? I have always loved him so much, you know."

"I thought," said Jared, "he was your husband now, Mummy."

The boys left on Boxing Day to join Richard in California, and Rena returned to London. That left me alone for most of the time on the forty-fourth floor. New York was like a ghost town over the holidays. I was miserable. I looked forward to Toronto, the first date on the sixteen-week tour, where I was to meet my cousin Margaret Moffett. We had been close friends since childhood; our family ties go back to 1764. She arrived the evening Rex was giving a party for the cast at a local restaurant. The weeks of rehearsal had taken their toll and Rex was at his most irascible. Clifford Williams, the director, had been wonderfully patient; producer Elliot Martin had ridden the storms and stalkings off with calm and tact. "The key to Rex," Moss Hart had once said, "is that he is not a frivolous man. He is the least frivolous actor I've ever worked with. What he gets he gets from digging, digging, digging." Once you understand that about Rex, you are able to forgive him a lot. Still it didn't do very much to ease the tension at home.

Rex was on edge the whole time. An unaccustomed voice was enough to set him off. When he heard me negotiating with a guitarist to play at the opening-night party in Toronto, he summoned me to the bedroom. What the hell did I think I was playing at? He pointed a long forefinger at the next room. Why had I invited that long-haired left-wing dropout into our suite? This crisp character reading was based solely on hearing the man's voice from the bedroom. The allegedly pot-smoking, long-haired Communist dropout was, in fact, a pleasant, middle-aged, short-back-and-sides professor of music who was to enthrall our guests with delicate renditions of "Greensleeves" and other medieval delights. Rex's temporary and rather fallible repose that night was tested by a society matron who gushingly informed him how lovely his performance was and, in the same breath, how much she admired his drip-dry shirt. He stared at the woman, trying to comprehend the full enormity of the remark. He was wearing, as usual, a silk shirt, designed and hand-made for him by Turnbull and Asser, the renowned shirt-makers of Jermyn Street, London. In the circumstances, he remained calm; stars, he told me once, are formed under great pressure—like diamonds. I now saw what he meant! I was never allowed to have his shirts laundered in the normal fashion; all his shirts were returned, at vast expense, to the shirtmakers to be cleaned.

While the play's teething troubles were being sorted out, Rex surprisingly gave me three days' leave of absence. I decided to see Quebec, then fly to New York for a couple of days with Margaret. We saw the sights of Quebec, the falling snow adding to the beauty. Unfortunately, the snow went on falling long after it had any aesthetic value. We were now stranded at the closed airport. It looked as if we were going to be snowed in for a long time. All the taxis had disappeared. At last an airline clerk took pity on us, and said he'd ring his friend who was a taxi driver and ask him to take us back to the hotel.

The driver arrived, casually dressed and wearing his bedroom slippers. He was, he explained, in a hurry to return home. His mother had his supper on the stove, and he wanted to watch the Frazier-Foreman fight on TV.

As soon as Margaret and I got into the car we started on the poor man, giving him our tale of woe, begging him to drive us to Montreal. He told us the road was impassable with snow, ice and fog, and that a bus from the airport had already run into trouble.

"Anyway," he said, "what about my mother's supper and what about the fight?"

His supper would keep, we assured him; the fight would most certainly be repeated. He gave in to our pleas and a fistful of dollars. Hours later we discovered Montreal Airport was also snowed in, the next train twenty-four hours away.

We asked the driver if he would care to take us to New York. He wasn't, he said, pointing to his bedroom slippers, suitably dressed for New York. We assured him they were the smartest bedroom slippers we had ever seen—slippers that could go anywhere. He counted the extra dollars thrust into his hand.

"Okay," he said, "but first I've got to call my mother and tell her to start supper without me."

The customs inspectors at Champlain greeted our little group with some incredulity. Our driver, never completely sold on our enthusiasm for his slippers, was determined to compensate for their shortcomings by stomping around in the snow with great vigor; no sound issued forth. The customs men waved us on, a look of wonderment on their faces.

As we continued on the road to New York, our driver told us he believed steadfastly in equality.

"If I can't sleep, then no one sleeps," he said, turning the radio up to deafening pitch. Margaret remarked it was quite an achievement to drive from Quebec to New York, and the only thing we managed to see en route was a blurred signpost saying "Vermont."

At daybreak we pulled into a truck drivers' café for breakfast.

"Hats on," ordered Margaret.

The driver didn't appreciate her remark as he looked despairingly at his bedroom slippers. We made a strange trio. I was sporting my silver fox again and Margaret was covered in mink.

After fourteen hours on the road we arrived at the Waldorf Towers. Our driver said a weary farewell; he was too tired to drive back to Canada that day. "I think I'll visit my auntie in Flatbush," he said.

On my previous visits to New York I had always been in the middle of some ghastly emotional crisis; because of that, I thought I hated the city. Now I saw it afresh with Margaret. Visiting the scene of the crime, Saks—or Ransaks as my brother Morgan now preferred to call it—I was unnerved when a saleswoman threw up her arms when I approached her.

"Christ Almighty," I said to Margaret, "don't tell me they still remember my last spree."

They didn't. It was Margaret who had impressed the assistant. "That voice," she screeched. "Just beautiful. I jess love it. It's the greatest when your Queen talks the King's English. You sound jess like her."

I was sorry when Margaret had to return to England.

Rex and I went on to Los Angeles for the second leg of the tour. The play opened in the 20th Century Plaza Theater. The auditorium was massive; backstage was just as big. There had been only one other show presented there and the whole building had an unlived-in feeling. Still it was impressively modern; the air-conditioning system along with the lights, sound, heating and everything else was controlled by computer. On opening night the computer somehow attached the air conditioning to the plumbing system; the audience was hereby informed every time a toilet was flushed or a tap turned.

Hollywood isn't a great theater town. Movie people, having to get up at the crack of dawn, usually retire early. But the opening night of *Henry IV* was as crowded with famous names as any opening I've ever seen in New York or London. The critics acclaimed Rex's performance. The worry and the sweat and the tears of the previous months had all been worthwhile.

We rented a small pretty house in Beverly Hills for the run of the play. We hired a black butler named Tosh. He was a marvelous character, not restrained by any very strict ideas of professional propriety, but far more pleasant than some other butlers I had come across. He wore a reddish curly wig that made no attempt to be convincing; his clothes were period dandy, although not necessarily all from the same period. Nevertheless, the overall effect was very smart and pleasing.

I enjoyed being back in California, a fact that surprised me a little bit. Friends were hospitable and warm; the country was beautiful and the way of life relaxing and seductive. Rex was still working out the problems with the play but even he seemed more at ease. One day when Rex had a matinee, I drove to Santa Barbara to have lunch with Paulene and Larry Harvey. He was directing and starring in a movie called *Welcome to Arrow Beach*. John Ireland and his wife Daphne were also there. Larry brought his own white wine together with baked potatoes and burnt toast for hors d'oeuvres. It reminded me of those luncheons we used to enjoy years ago at Elstree; only now I was married to Rex and Larry was married to Paulene. The lunch was marred by one thing; I was shocked by Larry's appearance. He looked pale and very drawn, although his energy and enthusiasm seemed as boundless as ever. I never ceased to be amazed by Larry's zest for life. I had no idea he was only months away from his death.

I stayed clear of the house I had shared with Richard in Bel Air; I was afraid it might trigger off bad memories. During our honeymoon trip around the world, Rex and I had stayed in Honolulu for a few days and I had foolishly got drunk and visited the house Richard and I had lived in on Diamond Head Road. It was a terrible mistake. My behavior that night upset Rex a lot. I had gone to the house to try to exorcise something inside of me, something I could never explain. Now, in California, I was taking no chances. I avoided the Villa Vesco like the plague. I knew I had been to the very edge of madness in that house. I was terrified of awakening the old chords. I sometimes feel that my body can take anything, but my mind is very vulnerable.

When it was time to leave California, we decided to keep on the invaluable Tosh; he would stay behind and pack up the house in Beverly Hills and join us in New York. He was delighted. When we got to Boston, Rex discovered he had left behind three hats, made for him by Hubert Johnson in London. I telephoned Tosh and told him to be sure to bring them with him to New York.

A few days later I received a telephone call from the

Los Angeles police. They wanted information on Tosh. There was very little I could tell them. "I can recommend him highly as a butler," I said.

"That won't do him much good now, lady," the detective said. "He's dead. He's been murdered."

I was stunned and upset.

When I told Rex what had happened he was shocked.

All day he was building toward eighty-thirty. Nothing else really mattered. "The only time I'm really happy," he said to me, "is the time I spend on stage in front of an audience."

Later Rex continued to astonish me with his singular view of life and death by saying, "Damn, now I suppose I'll never get my hats."

11. Farewell to Portofino

I tried to love Portofino. Villa San Genesio was the only home Rex ever really knew. He was proud of the fact that he and Lilli had built it together, had planned everything. It was a tribute to Lilli that the house, despite the upheavals of three successive wives, maintained the basic order she had established. She did more than organize the house, Rex admitted; she organized their social life, she made sure there were always plenty of people around to amuse and entertain him. Rex dislikes silence, avoids solitude—yet he is hopeless at organizing and planning his own days. His total lack of contact with people, his amazingly casual judgments are sometimes extraordinary. For twenty-one years he believed that one of his closest neighbors in Portofino was a Milan dentist; he was, in fact, one of the world's foremost maritime lawyers.

The days when everybody from the Duke and Duchess of Windsor to Greta Garbo dropped into the Villa San Genesio ended with the departure of Lilli. Rachel once gave me the visitors' book to sign and sighed, "Look at the rubbish we get here now compared with Lilli

Palmer's day." Since I was adding my name to the current roster of rubbish I felt a little wounded by her observation.

Rachel was jealous of Lilli's success as a social hostess; although I imagine Lilli would have had a hard time competing with Rachel's popularity among the people in the port. I doubt if there has ever been a more loved mistress of the Villa San Genesio than Rachel. She was warm, caring, outgoing and spontaneous. She had also bothered to learn Italian. She was, in a word, *simpatico*. I felt that locally I was held very much to blame for the breakup of her marriage to Rex. There was some prima-facie evidence to support that charge.

Once, when we had all been lunching in the port, Rachel abruptly stalked off in a rage, the cause of which completely mystified me and everybody else at the table. She had gone about twenty yards when she stopped and turned toward us. "Rex," she called in a belligerent voice, "come here. I want to talk to you." He followed her to the middle of the square; it was clear that a turbulent argument had started. It was Easter time; my brother Morgan and the boys were with me; we talked animatedly amongst ourselves, trying not to notice the glaring confrontation. Rachel ended the discussion by hitting Rex hard across the face and disappearing in the direction of the Gritta bar. Rex returned to our table. He was very upset.

The rumpus had drawn attention to him, and now people were surrounding our table, asking for his autograph, jostling each other trying to take his picture. I felt such a wave of pity for him at that moment.

Later an Italian magazine reported that I had been the cause of the fracas. I was not the cause. It was months before Rex and I were interested in each other.

Rex went less to the port after we were married. The locals blamed me for this, too. They said I was stuck-up and English. I was as Welsh as Rachel, of course, but I couldn't speak Italian. Neither could Rex. We sometimes had difficulty communicating with the servants and trades people. Rex had a guiltless, very English view of his linguistic limitations. "Christ, I've lived here for twenty-five years—you would think by now these bloody fools would have learned to speak English," he complained. Fortunately, his commanding manner usually translated very well in emergencies.

In the early days of our life together there, Rex had taken me on all his favorite walks and out for long trips in his Riva speedboat, which he loved. I had not noticed at first that our life in Portofino was both selfish and ominously self-contained. We were so involved with each other I had not realized just how isolated we had become.

We had no social contacts in the area at all. Nobody dropped in, nobody asked us over for drinks. Rex seemed incredibly vague about the surrounding life; he said all his friends had moved on, or were dead. It didn't appear to worry him very much; I think he regarded death and distance as much the same thing.

Isolation was a feature of the Villa Genesio. Cars could go only halfway up the hill; after that, there was a half-mile walk to a jeep for the final accent up the rough mule track to the villa. This haphazard approach was unforeseen when Rex had bought the land in 1949. Not until the villa had been completed did anyone point out to him that he had only pedestrian right-of-way. For a long time this had been no problem since nobody bothered to enforce the law; more recently villas had changed hands and gates had been erected. Our sense of estrangement from the rest of Italy was made more acute by the uncertainty of our water and electricity supply. We had no complaints about postal deliveries, garbage collection, laundry services or milk and bread deliveries—because there were none. Even the gas we used for cooking had to be hauled up the hill by the servants in giant bombolas. It was an ideal house for an ambitious handyman; Rex was inclined to shout at things when they broke down.

His standards were not lowered in any way. His excellent wine from his excellent cellar was always chilled to perfection. We had always to change for dinner, even when we dined à deux. Sometimes, when it was very warm, Rex would dispense with his jacket and wear a simple silk evening shirt. I was always expected, as were all women at his table, to wear a long dress. Any woman failing to comply with this requirement upset him dreadfully; it seemed to interfere with his precise sense of rhythm. The maids, in the most suffocating heat, wore stiff uniforms.

As I've said, I tried hard to love Portofino. The countryside was spectacular, the view from the house breathtaking, the port the prettiest I have ever seen. We invited friends to stay; the children spent their holidays there, often bringing school chums and their cousins Kate and Simon Moffett. I tried to make life there as normal as possible, but it was always a conscious effort and the lack of spontaneity was apparent.

The day began with the gardener hoisting the flag of St. George; this was a kingly signal that Rex was in residence. The shutters (firmly locked at night since the servants insisted banditti roamed the hillside) were opened at the same hour every morning, and the flowers watered to the exact minute every day. The house ran like clockwork. For a spell, at least, I brought life and animation to the place. I launched a villa festival with an Oscar for the best 8mm movie made by the children; there were darts tournaments, swimming galas, table-tennis championships. The house began to buzz with excitement. One evening, walking in the garden in the dusk, listening to the hubbub coming from the different rooms, Rex said to Gloria Lewis, "It's amazing the hidden life that goes on in different corners of a big house. I'm not used to it. I grew up in theatrical digs." Later when Gloria repeated that conversation to me, that sentence seemed to sum up my appeal for Rex. He saw my open house in Bedford Gardens, he saw my family and my friends and my casual, easygoing way of life. He thought that was what he wanted. When I finally gave it to him, he found it didn't suit him at all.

I amused myself studying the way our guests reacted to life at the villa. Most men seemed compelled to meet the challenge of walking all the way up the hill, shunning the jeep entirely. They usually did it just once. Richard Kershaw was one of the few men who actually seemed to relish the climb. Elaine and Peter Rawlinson loved the isolation; Gerald Savory sat pensively on the terrace longingly thinking of another terrace . . . the Carlton at Cannes; Michael Lewis would stare for hours in despair at the machine that was his lifeline: the telephone. Every morning, very early, he would begin battle with Italian operators in a bid to reach his broker in London; the Vuitton-clutching wife of an American agent did nothing to help her husband's negotiations with Rex by loudly admiring the grapes on the terrace—"They're so beautiful, just like our plastic ones at home!"

Dinner discussions were of the kind that usually required all-round apologies the next morning. I preferred to dine on the terrace, which was cool and uncluttered, in marked contrast to the sitting room; Rachel had brought to the sitting room a heavy air of Welsh respectability. Red velvet curtains and Welsh dressers seemed incongruous in the Mediterranean.

Now the big yachts usually bypassed Portofino for Sardinia, which had taken over as the favorite retreat of the jet set. Occasionally the Loel Guinnesses sailed in, once with Truman Capote on board. His soft cold hands and lisping voice disturbed me; I was pleased when he left. Sam Spiegel still brought his yacht in for a day or two now and again. He invited us all down for supper one evening to meet Lauren Bacall and Elsa Martinelli. Miss Martinelli wore a denim pants suit open to her navel at a time when no-bras were just coming into fashion: the men thought she looked stunning. Among the few regular visitors was Sir Isaiah Berlin, Fellow of All Souls, Oxford. He and his wife were old friends and neighbors of Rex and I looked forward to their visits. Isaiah walked for miles every day, his nose buried deep in some volume. He never stumbled and wore his own designed espadrilles with large lumps of cork sewn around the edges to prevent him stubbing his toes. He liked to boast he had a tenuous connection with show business. Winston Churchill had once confused him with Irving Berlin. "You can write a good tune, Mr. Berlin," the great man told him encouragingly.

But whoever called in on us, however amusing, however brilliant and stimulating, Rex would become restless toward the end of the summer. A sea trip was the only certain thing that would restore his humor.

One summer we chartered a palatial Greek yacht called *Candya*. The officers sent ashore to escort us aboard were unprepared for the group that met them: we looked more like a bunch of refugees than a grand yachting party heading for the Med. My cousin Margaret and her children had joined us. We had loaded a veritable tuck shop of goodies (Angel Delight to Rice Krispies) onto a wheelbarrow and proceeded to the port with our rowdy summer-kempt children in tow. The elegant Greek officers turned a paler shade of green. As was his wont on these family expeditions, Rex kept well out of the way. (His footwork at airports when he didn't want to be photographed with the children and an ocean of shabby luggage was every bit as nimble as anything Fred Astaire turned on for MGM.) This time he was viewing the whole operation from behind a protective bottle of champagne in Popestro's bar, an exclusive establishment above the port. I knew he would not show his face until the last packet of Angel Delight and the last bottle of Fairy Liquid was safely stowed away. I finally went to the Preporterous (a nickname inspired by the bills) and reported that all was ready for him to be piped abroad.

The magnificent *Candya* met with his approval—although the way the children were using the yacht's private helicopter for round-the-bay joy rides unnerved him quite a bit; it unnerved me, too, when I discovered that putting a helicopter down on a tossing deck was riskier than bringing in a Jumbo Jet at Heathrow.

Lacking guidebooks, we plotted a Napoleonic cruise from Volume N of the *Encyclopaedia Britannica*. In the harbor at Elba, crowds of photographers swarmed around the yacht, some clung to the rigging of nearby vessels trying to get intimate shots. I rather fancy we must have been a big disappointment to them. Even so, Constantine, our steward, discreetly lowered the canvas screens around the deck and we continued our exciting game of Twenty Questions. In a movie-star quiz, Jamie endeared himself to Rex forever by describing John Wayne as "almost middle-aged." That cruise was over far too quickly.

Rex said he never wanted to leave Portofino, and I understood that. But when one day he told me he would like to find a more accessible home in Europe I was delighted. We began to search for a house in the South of France . . . preferably on the road, ideally in the center of town! We found an Edwardian villa with a pretty garden overlooking the sea on the edge of Cap Ferrat. It had all we were looking for, including a swimming pool. Best of all, delivery vans came right up to the back door.

Rex doesn't waste time deliberating if he likes something. He immediately put in an offer which was immediately accepted.

We now had two homes in Europe. Complete with two sets of servants with whom we were unable to communicate. At least Cap Ferrat was a bit nearer home. I do get ridiculously homesick.

I welcomed our second home, although it meant a lot of extra work. Rex and I enjoyed decorating and planning the house together. He was most enthusiastic and could be seen wandering around with a paintbrush in one hand and a pot of paint in the other, with the gardener in hot pursuit with a large bottle of turps.

The rest of the year was spent getting into Beauchamp, our new villa. It was a hectic time. Rex had started work on his autobiography and was soon to begin rehearsals for the London production of *Henry IV*. Clifford Williams was again to direct, but this time it was to be a Bernard Delfont production with an entirely new cast. Rex was as apprehensive as he had been at the start of the American production.

As the weeks passed, he became more and more removed from me. It is strange how an atmosphere quickly communicates itself: instinctively friends stopped calling; the children no longer drifted into rooms where Rex might be. The whole relationship between Rex and the children, which had been affable and relaxed, underwent a disturbing change: they began to call him sir; they stood up whenever he entered the room. Sometimes I even found myself standing up when he entered the room.

It had also become second nature for me to open the door for him wherever he went. I realized things had got a bit out of hand when one morning in Harrods I leaped forward to hold open the door for several totally strange gentlemen.

Rex was in complete control; he dominated the house with his stifling and grandiose moods. It was a crushing blow to my hopes of a normal life together. I began to spend more and more time in bed; there seemed to be no good reason to get up. An accumulation of grievances, real and imagined, filled my head. I slumped deeper into my private world, into a treacherous isolation. I felt increasingly adrift. Our social life lacked the spontaneity I loved. However, very late one evening Rachel dropped in. She was in a reminiscent mood.

"Where did we go wrong, Rex?" she asked. "It was my fault."

"No, no," said Rex gallantly, "some of it was mine, surely?"

"Oh, I don't think so, luv," she said, embracing him in an absolving fashion.

"Do you want to know where we first made love?" she asked me in a confiding tone.

"Not really, Rachel," I said. Other people's intimate nostalgia had no appeal for me.

I decided to leave them to their oratorical memories. I retreated, locking the door firmly behind me. Some ten minutes later I had a desperate call from Rex on the intercom.

"For Christ's sake, Elizabeth, what the devil do you think you're up to, woman? Unlock this sodding door at once."

I could hear Rachel's irritation reaching a crescendo in the background. The recalled pleasure of yesteryear obviously had palled. This episode did nothing to resolve our differences.

My friends grew anxious. Maria St. Just confronted Rex. "I'm terribly worried about Elizabeth. She is so depressed. I have never seen anybody like this."

"Oh, I have," said Rex. "All my other wives."

We barely spoke to each other since conversations quickly degenerated into slanging matches—incoherent, violent, accusing, bitter—each making increasingly cruel accusations against the other. All the rules of civilized conduct were null and void. The feeling of groping at the edge of mental despair and darkness was frighteningly familiar to me. I seemed to have no control whatsoever over my life.

Sometimes I thought I was to blame. Perhaps I was just a spoiled bitch. Maybe I simply needed more love and attention than was fair to expect. I started drinking heavily again. I was scared.

Perhaps it was painful for Rex. I don't know. He is so very adept at hiding his true feelings behind actor's eyes. His outward attitude was one of indifference; he stood by and watched me going under.

Joan Thring was now married to Clifford Stafford, who was to become my hairdresser and my friend. They were endlessly kind, and patient with me. They suggested I needed a break, time away from Rex, to pull myself together, to gather strength, to see things in perspective. I thought that sounded sensible.

I decided to return to Los Angeles for a few weeks. I had friends there. More important, they were friends who knew nothing of the rift in our marriage and would not burden me with commiseration and advice.

It was on the plane to Los Angeles that I began to realize how far my depression had gone. I was so devitalized, so woebegone, I had no strength left to care.

There was fog in Los Angeles. The plane was diverted to San Francisco. When we landed I was taken into a small uncarpeted, sparsely furnished office. A Pan Am official was talking to me the way an adult might talk reassuringly to a lost child.

"You wait in here until you feel better," he was saying. "It's going to be all right. It's going to be just fine. There is nothing to worry about now."

I couldn't understand why he was talking to me in this way. Somebody was crying and sobbing in the next room, a woman was weeping and calling out uncontrollably.

It was a long time before I realized it was me.

I stayed with John and Daphne Ireland at their house in Santa Barbara. They were heroic. Never once did they complain about this self-invited house guest who would burst into floods of tears, or laugh too much at inappropriate moments. They tried to comfort me, but nothing worked. The one thing I wanted to work was my marriage. I desperately wanted to believe that it was all right; I tried to shut out all the doubts. I had to keep on the move: I felt that if I could exhaust my body, my mind would be at peace. In less than a week I was on my way back to London.

By now Rex had accepted that there was something seriously wrong with me as well as with our marriage. He was anxious to keep everything quiet. His attitude toward me now was both sympathetic and defensive. I did not want to return to Wilton Crescent and it was agreed that I should stay at the Berkeley Hotel for a week.

Rex visited me every day, trying to sort out our problems and our future. He finally agreed to let me take control of the household while he concentrated on his work. I told him I needed areas in which to function and to feel necessary; I also needed to see my friends and be able to invite people to the house freely. All this he agreed to.

"I have engaged a splendid couple," he told me the day I moved back into the house. "I'm sure you'll find them satisfactory—although I don't expect you will be staying very long." That was Rex all over!

The new butler, a large Spaniard without humor, took his role very seriously and my instructions with bad grace. The boys and I called him "A Butler" because when he answered the telephone he would intone the number and say, "A Butler speaking."

Rex was tremendously impressed with A Butler. Before he joined us, Rex was content to remain beneath the sheets while a maid brought us breakfast; now he rose early, and slipped into a silk dressing gown to await the arrival of his manservant bearing breakfast and *The Times*. It was apparent that A Butler brought out the patrician in Rex—or perhaps simply the born actor. Either way, Rex had become a master worthy of A Butler. It was a rewarding relationship and made them both very happy.

The only cloud on A Butler's horizon was the rest of us. The boys and I were clearly not in the same class as the master. One evening, while he was laying the table for Rex's supper, I had the temerity to take a plum from the bowl of fruit he had arranged on the dining table. A look of horror crossed his face. My teeth sank into the soft flesh a moment before his hand attempted to snatch it from my mouth. "Madam, they are the master's plums," he almost hissed. The incident was both funny and appalling: I decided to complain to Rex. He listened attentively to my story, a mandarin look of wisdom in his eyes. "I think a reprimand is in order," I concluded.

"Certainly not," Rex said, astonished at such a suggestion. "The man was perfectly correct, beloved. They *are* my plums."

After the opening of *Henry IV*, Rex invited the cast and some friends to a buffet party at the house. This was the first big party we had given with A Butler; I hired my old staff from Bedford Gardens to help out. It was the evening that A Butler's Latin sense of drama peaked. He was in a great state, screaming and shouting abuse and instructions at everyone in sight. This had very little effect, since in his great excitement he lapsed into Spanish, a language my Irish maids were not overfamiliar with; they found it difficult to follow the development of the scenario although they regarded A Butler with a good deal of interest.

During the evening I noticed a definite hiccup in the service—several of the late arrivals were without food; I hurried downstairs to investigate the holdup. I found A Butler in the middle of an animated dance in which he appeared to be imitating a saddened monkey. I dismissed the notion that it was some sort of demonstration concerning the Rock of Gibraltar. I waited for a further clue. I didn't have long to wait.

"Animals," he screamed, reverting to English. He thrust all his fingers rapidly in and out of his mouth. "Animals. They are all animals. They eat my food like starving animals. Every scrap, it is gone."

I realized at once he was referring to the eating habits of our guests. I saw that an admirable opportunity had arisen to put the man in his place. His behavior was clearly subversive to domestic discipline. I returned upstairs and suggested to Rex that he inform A Butler that social criticism of this sort was not part of his duties.

Rex descended the stairs with an unflinching alacrity that compelled respect. He watched the simian performance for several minutes. A Butler was undeterred by the presence of the master. He had obviously abandoned the old feudal spirit. Rex, for his part, had the unmistakable air of a man who has waited a lifetime to don the judicial black cap. I braced myself for the fireworks.

Rex spoke quietly and firmly. "You are quite right," he told the seething Spaniard. He then turned to me and said in a voice now filled with despair, "I told you never to invite actors to the house." He exited kitchen right, leaving the merest smell of greasepaint in the air.

In spite of his worthy master, A Butler finally decided it was time to move on. The rest of us, it seemed, were lowering the tone beyond redemption. The final scene, when it happened, happened quickly. It came during our preparations to embark for the South of France, where we were to spend the summer.

In view of the sometimes excessive heat in those parts, I suggested that A Butler might like to exchange his heavy black jacket for a linen one. He was shocked to the core. A look of anguish passed over his face. Clearly I had fallen even lower in his estimation.

He pulled himself up to his full height and said, "Pedro, A Butler—not Pedro, A Waiter."

He was out of the house before nightfall. I felt a bit on the stunned side, but happy. Rex brooded for weeks.

Rex was now working hard on his autobiography dur-

ing the day and appearing at Her Majesty's in the Pirandello play in the evenings. It was a hard schedule and
didn't do anything to improve our relationship. We had
become very unfriendly toward each other, even spite-
ful. The most dismal atmosphere prevailed in the house.
Despite his unparalleled preoccupation with his book and
the nightly demands of *Henry IV*, Rex was aware of our
alienation; he simply declined to comment on it.

"I must talk to you, Elizabeth. On a most urgent matter."

I drew a deep breath. I felt conscious of some impend-
ing crisis. I told him to go ahead.

He fidgeted. He cleared his throat. He put his hands in
his pockets. He took his hands out of his pockets. He had
that undefinable air of a man out for a stroll along a crumbling precipice.

"Elizabeth." He stared up at the ceiling. "Elizabeth, I
have to know now. What are your plans?"

"My plans, Rex?"

"Plans. For the future."

"The future?"

"Do you or do you not intend to leave me? I have to
know now."

He looked at his watch impatiently. I knew that time
was running out for our marriage; I had no idea that he
intended the countdown to be so precise.

"Why this minute, Rex? What is so very special about
this wet Wednesday morning?"

"Well, you see," he said. "I'm now up to the last chap-
ter in my book."

"Yes."

"It's about us. About you."

"Yes?"

"Well, dammit, Elizabeth, I have to know how to finish

the bloody thing. I can't leave us dangling in the air, can I? Are we going to be together when the book is published or aren't we?"

I laughed and loved him again. Of all the absolute clots, I thought. There are moments when he is beyond strategy. Most men would have simply lied. Rex in his single-mindedness couldn't see the outrageousness of what he had said. That is what makes him so vulnerable, I suppose, so infuriating, so impossible to live with, but finally so very beguiling.

At the end of the successful London run of *Henry IV*, Rex went to stay in France with a group of friends. I elected to stay on in London, for a few weeks. I thought that a short separation might improve things between us. The idiotic thing was, despite all the rows and the tension, at heart we both wanted our marriage to work. We still loved each other; there was nobody else in either of our lives. I was genuinely proud to be Mrs. Harrison—although Rex, unable to forsake the principles of a lifetime, had an unfortunate habit of treating me merely as the present holder of the title.

After a month I joined Rex at Beauchamp. His guests had departed and we were on our own. The trend of recent months alerted me to expect anything; I was ready for some tricky corners. But Rex was in an agony of remorse; he treated me with unremitting kindness. We behaved like lovers again, enjoying each other's company, content to be on our own. We lived for each day, not daring to think too far ahead, both desperately hoping. . . .

Good friends of mine, Gloria and David Rutherston, were giving a Gatsby Dance at their country home in Bisley, Gloucestershire. Gloria had arranged for me to stay as a house guest with a well-known M.P. for that area. I had not met him before but he was a most charm-

ing host and I invited him to a dinner party I was giving
in London a few weeks later.

At the end of that evening, he said he had something of
importance to say to me. He boiled down his case to a
few well-chosen words. He felt, he said, he had a good future in the Tory Party. He believed I might be an asset to
him—although he couldn't as yet be absolutely sure on
that point. I would be taken North to meet his family and
then be put "on appro," so to speak, for an unspecified period.

Since I was married at the time, it seemed a pretty
rummy proposal, or whatever. It was not the sort of thing
to spring on a lady after so short an acquaintance. I tried
to think of something to say, but nothing came. A girl
has to be a lot smarter than me to cope with a jolt like
that. I simply fixed him with a cold eye but it didn't
rattle him.

I felt that his remarkable offer called for some sort of
reply. I gave it a great deal of thought. In my garage was
a very large and very old four-poster bed, complete with
smelly drapes and mildewed mattress. I dispatched this
immediately to his small flat with a note thanking him for
his generous offer. The rest of my furniture, and my children, would be arriving shortly.

It would be idle to deny that the man's enthusiasm
waned abruptly.

They were lazy tranquil days. We would go to the local
market in Beaulien to hand-pick the fruit each morning.
Now I was allowed to share the plums! We would sit in
the small picturesque square, sipping cool local wine before lunch. No one bothered us. We enjoyed quiet intimate dinners high up in the hills on the Grand Corniche;
sometimes we settled for simple suppers in the little bis-

tros in one of the ports that were still comparatively uncrowded. We would wander through the flower market in Nice, wanting to buy everything for Beauchamp. It had a marvelous tranquillizing effect on my nervous system.

Rex announced he wanted to spend the remainder of that summer in Portofino. I confess that my heart sank. I never liked Portofino, although I did try for Rex's sake to grow fond of it.

There is always something in change, even the most longed-for change, that makes one sad. Perhaps it is because we always leave behind a little of ourselves. Now it was clear to me that Portofino was changing. I became aware of the uneasiness of the people around us. People seemed to walk slower, laugh less, no one seemed anxious to do anything any more. It was not the familiar Latin lethargy we knew; it was not even the indolence that overtakes all affluent resorts after a while. It was something oppressive, something bad. We could feel it even in the house.

Amando, our gardener and caretaker, was a strong youngish man who had lived in the villa for ten years with his wife Lucia. He was not a very friendly sort, but he was capable and was connected to a large family which provided us with a complete domestic service whenever we were in residence.

On our return this time I noticed that Amando's surly independence had taken on a more truculent tone. It seemed part of the general malaise of Portofino. In another hemisphere, in another age, I suppose one would have said that the natives were restive. Rex, perhaps, had not given this human drama the attention it deserved. When the crisis came he was totally unprepared.

For years it had been the custom for Amando to use the

jeep each morning to bring up the provisions; after midday it was left for Rex and his guests. Now the jeep was
often not available at all, and nowhere to be found. Rex
sent for Amando and asked why the old arrangement had
broken down. A quicker thinker than Rex would have
been hard put to anticipate Amando's response. A stream
of abuse poured out of him; one gets the meaning of certain words no matter what language they are spoken in.
To emphasize his Sicilian feelings, Amando engaged in
some lengthy and descriptive mime involving a stiletto
and large areas of Rex's person.

Anyone familiar with Rex's imperious temperament
will be surprised to learn that he held his tongue. Although to a sensitive man the spectacle of seeing one's
own jeep rudely purloined by one's gardener is pro-
foundly distressing.

A lawyer was engaged to settle the matter and act as
interpreter; Amando's miming skills were considerable
but rather too candid to accommodate the finer points of
Italian law. It transpired that the local Communist
commissars would deal with it for Amando.

The commissars came to the villa to supervise the talks.
They were large men in short baggy trousers and porkpie
hats. They roamed through the villa inspecting everything, including us, with unnecessary thoroughness. Rex
was magnificently aloof. But it was clear that our days at
Portofino were numbered. A $7,000 payoff was finally
agreed to. It was also discovered that the wily Amando
had registered the jeep in his own name; Rex had no legal
claim to it whatsoever.

Although one of nature's arch conservatives, Rex has
never held any strong party political views. "On the
whole," he said to me once, "I prefer to exist splendidly."
The obvious class envy of the commissars distressed him;

he was not taken in by their ideological bullshit. "How can they be true Communists when they take ten percent? That is an agent's cut. It is illogical. All agents are capitalists," he said.

He put on a brave front, but I felt immensely sorry for him. It was such an unhappy farewell to a place he loved so much. More than twenty-five years of his life had been spent in that villa; if it is possible for any actor to put down roots, he put his down in the soil of Portofino. And now this.

With Amando gone, we lost the rest of our staff. I was now head cook and bottle washer. Rex did his best to adapt to the new arrangements. Every morning after he had bathed, shaved, cleaned his teeth and carefully dressed, he always without fail filled the ice trays. Unfortunately he always omitted to close the refrigerator door. He hates to close any door. "It seems," he say, "so final."

Terence Rattigan and producer Arthur Cantor chose this time to call on us to discuss Terry's new play, *In Praise of Love*, which Rex was to do in New York in November. Apart from all our other difficulties, *In Praise of Love* raised a particularly delicate subject. It was the story of a young woman dying of an incurable disease; her husband knows but must hide the facts from her. Rattigan told us straight out that he had based the play on Rex's experience with Kay Kendall. I am certain that Rex would not have considered the play for a moment had it not been written by Terry. Terry had written Rex's first London stage success, *French Without Tears*, and they had remained close friends ever since. Rex trusted his taste and craftsmanship completely. This time I wasn't too convinced about his taste, but there was very little I could say that wouldn't sound churlish. I was in an impossible position. Our marriage was too fragile to bear too much truth. When Rex asked me whether I thought he should play the part, I raised no objections. I was not convinced that any objections I might have raised would have been listened to. Terry was sensitive enough not to twist Rex's arm, but he didn't have to: Rex saw the potential of the role at once.

Meanwhile, I had other things on my mind. With no staff, the house was vulnerable to burglars and any further demands that might be made from the Left. I decided to pack up our more valuable possessions and take them to Beauchamp. Rex informed me he had already taken all the clothes he wanted to keep; the rest could be left for the peasants on the mule track, he said with cheerful charity. On close inspection of his wardrobe, I discovered there remained only several dinner jackets, a suit of tails and a variety of velvet smoking jackets. As mule tracks go, ours was quite an informal one and the peasants rarely changed for dinner.

12. *If at First . . .*

At the end of that summer, Rex left for New York to begin rehearsals for the Rattigan play. He had been working on the play during our last weeks at Beauchamp; the doubtless biographical material, the constant reference to the dramas of his past, the harping on his love for Kay, did nothing to alleviate the uneasiness of our situation. The closeness we had found during our early days alone in Beauchamp had faded, leaving behind the unhappy couple of Wilton Crescent. I could almost hear our marriage ticking.

With Rex again embarking on the rigors of rehearsal, I had plenty of time for reflection. I thought how very odd it is that we seem to keep learning the same lessons, the same truths, under different labels. I had already found that love does not conquer all. That loving someone and being loved by them is not enough to make a marriage work, yet here I was again. Who was it said that love's nature's second sin? Did that apply to actors? I wondered. A wife is no great asset to an actor. Actors cannot be family men, cannot be husbands in the way one is brought up to expect husbands to be. On the surface, acting has become a respectable profession, emblazoned with peerages and knighthoods and Empire Medals, but essential roguery is still there.

For stardom, Rex had fought and, if I have understood his correctly, bled. "It is such a ruthless lark, stardom," Larry Harvey once said to me. That seems to sum it up fairly well. Forced by ambition and ego to be a loner, a star must dominate and overpower those around him—rivals, co-stars, directors, even friends and relations. It is more than a game; it is a need. Richard had it; Rex had it. You enter their world as an intruder. In each case I fell in love with the man only to see him disappear into the actor. When that happens, the game is up.

The Rattigan play fascinated Rex, but the reminder of events and passions of seventeen years before also unsettled him. He called me every day from New York, but our conversations were stilted and tense and often ended with one or other of us slamming down the receiver. Before I had always made the excuse to myself that the demands of rehearsing a new play or learning a new part had caused the strain in our marriage and that the rift would be mended once the play had opened, or the movie finished. This time I knew that Rex's career had nothing to do with our personal problems.

I had agreed to go to New York for the opening of *In Praise of Love*. If I had not gone it would have looked like petulance, as if I were jealous of Kay Kendall. By going I knew I was submitting myself to an ordeal; everybody in that first-night audience knew what was happening up there on that stage: Rex reliving his last months with Kay. Voyeurism is not my strong suit and I knew I would feel uncomfortable, to say the least.

Rex knew how I felt but insisted he needed my support

on opening night. He came to Kennedy Airport to meet me. There is something grandly ambassadorial about Rex in a crowd. He wore a dark blue fur-lined overcoat with a velvet collar. I saw him at once standing in that familiar attitude of negligent hauteur made for the drawing room, which is clearly his native element. With his public air of *gravitas,* one instinctively recognizes him as an Englishman of breeding.

However angry I have been with Rex, however fierce and brazen the rows, I always get the same sensation whenever we are about to meet again. My heart seems to lurch literally into my throat. This anatomical aberration did not last long at Kennedy; Rex was in a beastly mood.

He had taken a suite in the Regency Hotel for the run of the play and we entertained many old friends. But opening night came and went and still I had not met a single member of the cast; he gave an opening-night party at the "21" and didn't ask any of the cast. I suggested this deserved a mention of some kind in *The Guinness Book of World Records.* He was not amused.

I returned to England to spend Christmas with my children; Rex had two performances on Christmas Day and did not unduly mind. I returned to New York in January, full of apprehension. Rex was at his most charming when we met. Unfortunately, his supply of charm was running low; within a few days we were desperately unhappy again, and fighting again. I know now that our days were numbered. Sometimes Rex recognized it, and sometimes he didn't. It was uncanny how after a blazing row he could pick up the telephone and talk to me as if the whole thing had never happened. We were now spending more time apart than together, and the excuses were becoming more facile. Yet he could still, from a distance, amuse me a lot with his unconscious humor and I loved him for that. Once he asked me to join him in Paris for a black-tie party at Maxim's. I declined. The following evening, the evening of the party, he telephoned to say he was feeling rather unwell. "How the hell," he wanted to know, "does one get an aspirin in this town?"

"What a pity, Rex," I commiserated. "You'll miss Maxim's."

"Oh, I shall probably go," he said in his world-weary voice. "Only I shalln't wear a black tie."

The year 1975 was not a good one for Rex and me. Our separations became more frequent and more serious; the goodbyes hurt and the reconciliations became less able to ease the pain.

I took an apartment in Belgrave Place, and was promptly burgled. Rex, with his remarkable sense of timing, telephoned me from Paris at the precise moment I had discovered the burglars helping themselves to my jewelry. They pushed past me in the hall as the telephone rang.

"Elizabeth," Rex said, coming to the point at once. "I'm in a frightful tizz."

"So am I," I said. "I've just been robbed."

"How do I get all this luggage to the South of France?"

"They seem to have cleaned me out," I said, quite dazed.

"I'll never cope with this lot," he said. "I do detest traveling by myself."

"My favorite pieces have gone," I said.

"What am I going to do? I have seven pieces of luggage."

"The porters at the Lancaster are not unfamiliar with luggage," I said icily. "I must call the police."

He sighed. "At least," he said, "you've got something positive to think about."

The following day the story of the burglary appeared in the newspapers. It had been a fairly hefty haul and Rex was on the telephone to me at once. His voice was thick with concern.

"Darling, I've just seen the newspapers. I'm shocked. It really has only just sunk in. . . ."

I assured him I was perfectly all right; no one, thank God, had been hurt. His shock, however, was of a different kind.

"Damn it, darling, I had no idea I had given you so much jewelry," he said, stunned by his own generosity. Rex had been generous, but generosity between a man and a woman is measured in many different ways, not all of them tangible.

Unguarded and careless to a degree hardly credible, Rex has never ceased to astonish me. There are lots of people who feel that his talent forgives everything, among them Rex. Repeated forgiveness is, however, a hollow sensation. After many reconciliations I finally left Rex in July 1975. I felt very low. I still loved him and he loved me, but we were simply destroying each other.

We were divorced in December in a makeshift lean-to, a temporary court of the overloaded High Courts. How very strange, I thought, that a marriage that had started in such a grand and glamorous way should end in this small, seedy room, barely large enough to hold all the legal representatives.

Nevertheless, I think the most encouraging thing about my life is that it has always been unpredictable. I wouldn't want to change that. I have spent more than half my life with two very strong men. In order to survive as an individual I had to leave them. I learned from them lessons in determination, pride and forgiveness. I also learned the importance of independence.

Rex and Richard in their different ways made me realize the necessity of being my own person.

"Not every end is the goal. The end of a melody is not its goal, and yet if a melody has not reached its end, it has not reached its goal."
—Nietzsche